SOFT C

SOFT OPTIONS
For Adults Who Have Difficulty Chewing

Rita Greer

SOUVENIR PRESS

First published 1998 by
Souvenir Press Ltd,
43 Great Russell Street, London WC1B 3PA

ISBN 0 285 63447 X

Typeset by Rowland Phototypesetting Ltd,
Bury St Edmunds, Suffolk

Printed in Great Britain by
The Guernsey Press Company Ltd,
Guernsey, Channel Islands

Contents

	Introduction	7
1	Nutrition	11
2	Balanced Diet and Healthy Eating	19
3	Cooking Equipment and Techniques	28
4	Bread and Basics	46
5	Breakfasts and Juices	70
6	Sauces, Gravies and Dressings	85
7	Soups and Starters	94
8	Salads, Vegetables and Vegetarian Dishes	109
9	Main Meals	125
10	Puddings and Desserts	145
11	Cakes and Teatime Food	160
12	Treats and Celebration Food	167
13	Packed Meals, Picnics, Sandwiches and Snacks	178
14	Drinks, Preserves and Garnishes	191
	Appendices	200
	Main Meal Suggestions	200
	Conversion Tables	202
	Useful Addresses	203
	Index	204

Introduction

One of the first observations an archaeologist makes when confronted by a skull concerns the teeth still left in the jaws. The skull may be thousands of years old, yet by studying the teeth it is possible to say how old the person was at the time of death and how healthy he or she would have been.

As our teeth serve us on a daily basis from about the age of five, quite naturally they become worn down with use, particularly the large teeth (the molars) at the sides of the jaw, top and bottom, which grind food to a paste. If the archaeologist sees that some teeth are missing from the skull and that those remaining are in a badly worn state, it will be obvious their owner did not enjoy good health. He or she would probably have fallen prey to deficiency and degenerative diseases through being unable to chew properly. (A link with worn-down teeth is often visible signs of arthritis in the joints of the limb bones, and signs of abscesses in the jaws.)

In the animal kingdom, mammals that are unable to chew become sick and die. However, it is possible for humans to live a long time after their teeth have gone, thanks to the skill of dentistry and by selecting and preparing appropriate food.

The chronic illnesses of old age often have their roots in poor nutrition during earlier years. It is a legacy that cannot usually be rectified, especially for degenerative illness. One can only wonder how much illness is due to the middle-aged chewing less efficiently and the elderly not chewing at all. With a growing percentage of people over 65 years old and many of us living to our 80s and 90s, the number of people who might do well on 'soft options' food increases yearly.

Necessity is frequently the mother of invention, and when faced with caring at home for my husband who was unable to chew and who had spent years in hospitals and nursing homes I felt I had been thrown in at the deep end. Unable to find a suitable cookbook and knowing how the standard 'soft diet' had failed him, I had no choice but to face the serious nature of the problem and set about experimenting and trying to understand the implications of such a regime. Coping alone at home gave me first-hand experience.

What I had witnessed while visiting hospitals and nursing homes over four years was a curious mixture of kindness and cruelty. I saw some staff go to endless trouble to help patients back to health, and their seemingly uncaring colleagues who couldn't wait for their shift to end. Some incidents stick in the memory, like the day I saw a blind and disabled man who couldn't hold a spoon, trying to feed himself with red jelly by attempting to pick it up with his crippled hands. I had missed a similar occurrence at breakfast when he had tried to do the same with porridge because there was nobody available to feed him.

I saw many patients who couldn't chew properly given the most inappropriate food—leathery sandwiches, tough meat, spaghetti . . . I remember cutting up food for a man who was unable to speak but could roar. And roar he did, for he was unable to use his hands to feed himself and had to sit looking at the salad he had been given.

Eventually a report was published, suggesting that patients in hospital might not be properly nourished, either because their food was unsuitable or because they couldn't feed themselves. As a good deal of food ends up in the waste-bin for one reason or another, it would be appropriate if there was new thinking on the subject. I have to admit that the patients I saw in hospital who were happiest with their food were those whose relatives brought in a regular supply. (My husband ended up with a gastric tube and I ended up with depression.)

The obsession with the calorie since the Second World War has led to a belief that calories are actually a kind of food. This in turn leads to indiscriminate food selection and the ultimate unbalanced diet. When this is coupled with not chewing the food, several problems can arise: indigestion, reflux, wind, pain, constipation and malnutrition. Instead of restructuring the diet to cope with these, the traditional answer has been to put even more into the stomach in the form of pills.

Convenience foods came into their own after the last war, when many more women had to go out to work as well as bring up a family. Caring has largely had to change to just coping and convenience food

8

is now the norm. As long ago as the early nineteenth century, women were advised to cook meals which were wholesome, economical and nourishing. Now the buzz words are 'fast', 'instant', 'easy' and 'quick'. Convenience seems to be for the cook and overrides the nutritional good of the family. At home, as well as in institutions, we seem to be going backwards in our attitude to food.

The very nature of institutional management results in cheap and easy food, preferably bought in ready to serve. For a soft diet this usually means just a few foods appearing on the menu with monotonous regularity—yoghurt, reconstituted mashed potato, ice-cream, custard, porridge and stewed apple, overcooked or canned mashed vegetables, mashed fish or fishcakes. When the patient fails to respond well to this boring selection and begins to lose weight, out comes the liquid milk-based food. At home the usual solution is to mash or liquidise the food eaten by the rest of the household. This can be an unhappy solution, either because the food is unsuitable for this process or because the patient feels the food has been changed in such a way as to render it inferior to that eaten by everyone else.

However the problem is tackled, 'baby-food' seems to creep back on to the menu, disappointing and depressing the adult patient and often failing to provide adequate nourishment.

Common sense indicates that what is needed is a completely new cuisine, designed for adults and taking into account the wide variety of food normally consumed—vegetables and fruit, salads, bread and bakery items, cereals, meat, fish, poultry, eggs, cheese and so on. Balance is just as important as for an ordinary diet, or even more so, and this cannot be achieved by using just a few convenience foods.

As I experimented on my willing patient, I began to understand that I could compensate for lack of variety in texture by making more effort with taste and presentation. I saw too the value of the excitement generated by new and better food when foods previously enjoyed had to be taken off the menu. Gradually, mealtimes which had been dreaded turned into events eagerly awaited. Pleasurable anticipation replaced lack of appetite and disappointment. With appetite stimulated and food once more a pleasure and easily digested, the result was a great improvement in health and strength.

It is easy to arrive at a poor state of health, totally unfit and with low esteem. Just don't eat sensibly or properly and it doesn't take long. Once depression has set in, the task of getting well becomes doubly difficult: people lose heart and go downhill. 'An army marches on its stomach', but even without a war situation, life is a battle for most of us. How much better can we cope if we are properly nourished?

Living on food that doesn't need chewing may seem a strange change of direction at first. People expect it to be like baby-food, bland, boring and repetitious. It need not be anything like that. When it comes to eating, the jaws will be permanently on holiday. Not having to chew can be felt as a relief after chewing has become not just an inconvenience but an impossibility.

Soft options cuisine has a style all its own. It is a recognisable kind of food with a great sense of purpose. Those who wish to be flamboyant can extend the style with bold garnishes, and inspiring presentation. There is nothing second-best about soft options cuisine, in fact it is special as it focuses on a special need. I hope this book will be of help to both carers and the cared-for.

CHAPTER 1

Nutrition

The human body needs to take in food to survive. This involves eating, (chewing and swallowing) and digesting to ensure energy, movement, heat, growth, repair, maintenance and (possibly) reproduction.

Digestion is a complicated business whereby the body processes the food so that the nutrients can be extracted and waste material passed out. To function properly the body needs to put the nutrients into the bloodstream so that they can be carried to wherever they are needed.

Food enters the body via the mouth, and it is here that a vital job must be performed—that of transforming large pieces of different foods into a kind of wet paste, ready for pushing down to the stomach. Strong muscles in our jaws power teeth for biting, tearing and grinding; the tongue pushes the food about so that it can be chewed quickly. Glands in the mouth produce saliva to lubricate the food and make chewing easy.

Chewing

You can see how important it is for food to be chewed before going down into the stomach. If it is not chewed properly, all kinds of problems may arise—difficulty in swallowing, choking, indigestion, reflux, heartburn, pain, discomfort, wind, constipation, poor absorption of vitamins and minerals and so on.

There are several reasons why adults may not chew properly—

11

badly aligned jaws which prevent use of teeth, badly aligned teeth (wrong bite), worn-down teeth, teeth missing due to extraction, decayed teeth, wear and tear of old age, dental work, poorly fitting dentures, no teeth or dentures at all, illness, weakness, frailty, pain, paralysis, the result of a stroke, Bell's palsy or surgery, gum disorder, mouth ulcers, sore tongue or gums, sore or cracked lips, sore throat. While some of these problems are temporary and can be attended to or cured, others cannot and the problem and inconvenience are lifelong.

Although the toothless baby or toddler can grow a set of teeth, adults cannot; the last set we grow (after our milk teeth have gone to the tooth fairy), has to last anything up to ninety-five years. Even when chewing is difficult or impossible, food still has to be sent down to the stomach as a digestible wet paste. Non-chew food is the answer, the 'soft option'.

Appetite

There is an important factor to consider in connection with digestion and that is appetite. This is what makes us want to eat, and by stimulating the appetite with the sight, smell and taste of food the process of digestion starts. In particular the salivary glands must be activated: 'mouth-watering' as a description of food is a great compliment. If food does not appeal to the senses in some way, digestion is not stimulated. It is always worth taking trouble to present food attractively, especially if it is a new kind.

Many people jump to the conclusion that liquidised food is the answer for soft options foods and find it off-putting. In fact the smooth texture produced by liquidising or blending is only suitable for drinking. It is acceptable for juices and soups, not for eating, and it is quite different from non-chew food.

FOOD

Most adults live on what is called a 'mixed diet' of meat, fish, eggs, milk and dairy products, grains, fats and oils, vegetables, fruit, nuts, sugar and beverages. Vegetarians avoid meat and fish; vegans avoid all animal products. There are also exclusions which vary according to particular religions, or to medical diets or foods.

By eating too little, or not at all, even if hunger pangs signal that it is time to do so, the risk is malnutrition. Persistent periods of eating too little or no food lead to starvation and eventually death. By eating too much a person becomes overweight and then obese.

Due to continual overeating, the extra food taken in turns to stored fat. The body has difficulty in moving and functioning and even the most basic movements such as walking can become extremely difficult and painful; breathing becomes laboured and the person grows larger and weaker as the overeating continues. (Elvis Presley appears to have suffered in this way.)

There are six basic types of nutrients found in a mixed diet. Carbohydrates are needed for energy and to keep the body warm. Fats are another high energy source. Proteins are needed for repair and growth but can also be used for energy and heat. Vitamins, minerals and trace elements are all required for efficient working of the body, and to obtain them it is important to eat a wide variety of foods.

VITAMINS AND MINERALS

These are the main vitamins, minerals and other trace nutrients and the foods that contain them.

Vitamin A for healthy bones, hair, eyes, skin and teeth. In fish, oils from fish liver, green and yellow fruit and vegetables, carrots, spinach.

Vitamins B1, B2, B6 and B12 (vitamin B complex)—for healthy eyes, food canal, brain, ears, heart, nervous system, nails, liver, skin, blood, muscles, gall bladder, glands, tongue. B1 in brewer's yeast, wheatgerm, wholegrain, yoghurt; B2 in brewer's yeast, eggs, fruit, green vegetable leaves, beans, nuts, wholegrain, poultry; B6 in avocado pear, bananas, brewer's yeast, cabbage, fish, green vegetable leaves, prunes, raisins, walnuts, wheatgerm; B12 in beef, eggs, milk products, fish, pork, cottage cheese.

Vitamin C—for healthy adrenal glands, blood, skin, ligaments, bones, gums, teeth, heart. In fresh fruit and vegetables.

Biotin—for cell growth, making fat, helping to use protein, fat and carbohydrate in the body. In brewer's yeast, egg yolks, beans and wholegrains.

Choline—for healthy liver, gall bladder and nerves. In brewer's yeast, egg yolk, fish, beans, soya, wheatgerm.

Folic acid—for the appetite, reproduction, circulation, liver function, red blood cell formation. In oranges, lemons, green vegetable leaves, milk products, seafood, wholegrain.

Inositol—helps to stop hardening of the arteries, reduces cholesterol, helps the body to use fat and grow hair. In brewer's yeast, oranges, lemons, meat, milk, nuts, vegetables, wholegrain.

13

SOFT OPTIONS

Pantothenic acid—helps to remove toxic substances, may help hair to keep its colour, activates friendly bacteria in the food canal, helps the body to use protein. In brewer's yeast, eggs, beans, mushrooms, salmon, wheatgerm, wholegrain.

Pangamic acid—helps breathing and encourages the glands and nervous system to work, helps the body to use protein, fat and sugar. In brewer's yeast, brown rice, sunflower and sesame seeds, wholegrain.

Vitamin D—for healthy bones, heart, nerves, skin, teeth, thyroid gland. In egg yolk, milk, fish, fishbones.

Vitamin E—for healthy blood vessels, heart, lungs, nerves, skin. In butter, vegetables with dark green leaves, eggs, fruit, nuts, vegetable oils, wheatgerm.

Vitamin F (polyunsaturates)—for healthy cells, glands, hair, nerves, skin. In safflower, sunflower, corn and soya oils, wheatgerm, sunflower seeds.

Vitamin K—for healthy blood and liver. In vegetables with green leaves, safflower oil, yoghurt, oats.

Vitamin P (bioflavonoids)—for healthy blood, skin, gums, ligaments, bones and teeth. In fruits including the skins, apricots, grapes, cherries, grapefruit, plums, lemons.

Calcium—for healthy bones, blood, heart, skin, teeth. In milk, cheese, yoghurt, almonds.

Chromium—for healthy pancreas and glucose metabolism. In brewer's yeast, corn oil, wholegrain cereals.

Copper—for healthy blood, bones, circulation, hair, skin. In beans, nuts, seafood, raisins, avocado, liver, soya, beansprouts, watercress, parsley.

Iodine—for hair, nails, teeth, thyroid gland. In seafood, seaweed.

Iron—For healthy blood, bones, nails and skin. In eggs, fish, wheatgerm, poultry, liver, dark green vegetables, spices.

Magnesium—for healthy arteries, bones, heart, muscles, nerves, teeth. In wheat bran, honey, vegetables, nuts.

Manganese—for healthy brain, muscles, nerves. In bananas, wheat bran, celery, cereals, egg yolks, vegetables with green leaves, liver, nuts, wholegrain, pineapple.

Phosphorus—for healthy bones, blood, brain, nerves, teeth. In eggs, fish, grains, meat, poultry, liver.

Potassium—for healthy blood, heart, kidneys, muscles, nerves, skin. In dates, figs, peaches, tomatoes, raisins, seafood, sunflower seeds.

Selenium—for immunity and cell production. In fish, meat, eggs, wholegrains, brown rice.

14

Sodium—for healthy blood, muscles and nerves. In salt, milk, cheese, seafood. (Most of us take in 20 to 30 times more salt than we need.)

Zinc—for healthy blood, heart. In brewer's yeast, liver, seafood, soya, mushrooms, sunflower seeds, spinach.

The list shows the vitamins and minerals we know about, but doubtless there are more waiting to be discovered and understood.

Antioxidants

These are important for preventing cell degeneration. Foods contain a vast number of antioxidant substances, including vitamins A, C and E. There are more of these vitamins in fresh food than in highly processed food, as well as bioflavonoids and other important 'friendly chemicals'. It may well be that degenerative conditions including ageing are kept at bay by a diet rich in these substances. Fresh fruit and vegetables are the best source.

Fibre

Cleansing and waste disposal foods are the high fibre foods such as wholewheat flour and bread, brown rice, potato skins, leafy greens, beans and fruit skins.

Fibre is a non-food but nevertheless important in the diet. It has been known for decades that waste disposal from the body is more inclined to be a regular event when a diet high in fibre is consumed. In spite of this knowledge, the usual method of promoting regularity is to administer laxatives rather than to increase dietary fibre. Although laxatives might seem to solve the problem temporarily, in the long term they can be bad news for the colon.

Water

Liquid is very important in the diet as it is required to ease the passage of food through the digestive tract. Without liquid it is possible to die within hours and in many languages the word for water also means life. Cutting down on liquids to prevent water building up in the tissues is a common practice among slimmers, but this is probably better controlled by not taking too much salt which can encourage bloating.

Absorption

When food goes into the stomach it needs to be in a form that enables the stomach to deal with it. If it has not been properly chewed the body will be unable to extract the nutrients it needs. The farther down the digestive tract the food goes, the more opportunities are missed for absorption. By the time it is passed out of the body as waste it will hardly have changed and the nutrients will be lost. As the body ages it tends to absorb nutrients less efficiently, and there are also some medical conditions which result in poor absorption—coeliac disease, irritable bowel syndrome (IBS) and allergies. They may be a lifelong problem for some people.

Continual malabsorption leads to malnutrition, deficiency diseases and poor health. Tackling old age or illness with this extra problem can only make matters worse. Supplementing the diet with vitamins and minerals can be a help, but there's nothing better than obtaining these vital nutrients from fresh food.

MALNUTRITION

Malnutrition can result in failing health and strength, eye problems, anaemia, scurvy, rickets and vitamin deficiencies. The teeth become loose, gums bleed, hair falls out, skin develops rashes, there is weight loss, weakness and apathy. It is not a pleasant picture.

Old people living alone tend to eat poorly and can respond with a great improvement in health and well-being when properly fed by someone else. Those too weak or unmotivated to feed themselves become malnourished even when food is readily available. This is known to happen in hospitals and institutions where understaffing is a problem and where nutrition is still not recognised as a major controlling factor regarding good health and swift recovery from surgery or illness.

There are ten basic causes of malnutrition, including those already mentioned. However, they should be considered with the other causes for a balanced view.

Common causes of poor nutrition
In some parts of the world famine is still the main single cause of malnutrition. Plagues of pests, drought or flood lead to crop failure and there is simply not enough food to go round. In the developed countries there is plenty of food—in fact far too much. In spite of this people still suffer from deficiencies for many reasons:

1 *Poor quality food.* Usually this is due to overprocessing and long storage.
2 *Poverty.*
3 *Ignorance.* The average person's knowledge of suitable diet and

nutrition for a particular lifestyle is extremely poor. This is so right across society.

4 *Anorexia.* Boredom, depression and inertia tend to decrease the appetite. Elderly, retired people, especially those living alone, are prone to this, but it is also widespread among young people who carry the slimming obsession to extremes.

5 *Dental problems.* Being able to chew food properly is a necessary part of digestion. Missing teeth, dental caries, gum disorders and mouth infections account for some poor eating habits, particularly in the elderly. If eating becomes painful instead of pleasurable, then food is avoided.

6 *Poor digestion.* This is sometimes caused by absorption defect diseases which may not be severe enough for diagnosis. Some people, on the other hand, suffer from poor digestion causing flatulence, heartburn, and indigestion. These are common ailments.

7 *Chronic diseases.* People suffering from chronic disease need the very best nutrition. All too often loss of appetite and poor care result in poor nutrition.

8 *Ageing.* Like everything else, our bodies eventually wear out. Elderly people may not be able to secrete as much gastric juice or produce enough enzymes for digestion as they did when younger.

9 *Apathy.* Lack of energy, incentive and imagination can lead to loss of interest in food. Preparing proper meals becomes too much trouble, resulting in a poor standard of nutrition. Shopping, with the advent of the supermarket and self-service store, has become more difficult compared with the days when orders were delivered to people's homes. Some people would rather go without food than face shopping for it, particularly those living in cities.

10 *Fads.* Slimming, imaginary or real food allergies, religious or conscience cults can lead to peculiar dietary balances. Combined with poor knowledge of nutrition, this can lead to deficiencies.

Sensible diet for health
Everyone needs to eat the right mixture of foods to ensure sufficient nutrients for the life they lead. The average diet contains too much sugar, fat and salt but not enough fruit and vegetables or fibre.

Pleasure
What makes us want to eat? We all have a basic instinct to eat for survival but pleasure in food is important even if there are difficulties. The clever approach is to overcome the difficulties and keep hold of the pleasure. There is also the aspect of comfort. People who cannot chew require special food to survive—every day. When this is prepared for them (or they prepare it themselves) and they can eat it easily, it both comforts and reassures. Above all, it nourishes them and makes them healthy.

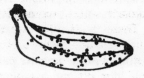

CHAPTER 2

Balanced Diet and Healthy Eating

What usually happens when a person has to follow a non-chew diet is that any food which is a problem to chew is automatically dropped from the list. With so many foods requiring processing or special attention to make them non-chew, the majority are avoided, thus severely unbalancing the diet. The result is poor nutrition which in turn leads to deficiency disease and illness, to say nothing of lack of interest in food.

Think of a pair of old-fashioned scales. On one side (where the weights are placed) is good health and on the other side, in the scalepan, is the selection of foods that make up the diet. When the food selection is mostly wrong it won't balance with good health.

We know which kind of foods will possibly ruin our health if we eat too much of them:

- too much sugar, fat and salt; too much cream, butter, margarine;
- too many fried foods, cakes, biscuits, pastries, sugary puddings, ice-cream;
- processed/junk food, salty food and snacks.

We also know that by filling ourselves up with the wrong foods we won't have room for some of the right foods for good health. These are fresh fruit and vegetables including greens, foods with natural fibre, foods low in salt, sugar and fat.

19

The average 'soft diet' at home comprises rice pudding, ice-cream, yoghurt, jelly, 'baby food', porridge, omelette, mashed potato, banana, steamed fish and scrambled egg. Whatever happened to salads, greens, vegetables, bread, pasta, fresh fruit and a variety of high-protein foods?

Suggested minimum food intake for one person per week

This is to give you some idea of what an ordinary, healthy diet looks like on paper. It is followed by basic solutions for making the foods suitable for a soft options diet.

Milk (preferably skimmed or semi-skimmed)—2 pints (1 litre).
Eggs—3.
Fats and oils—margarine (polyunsaturated) under 3oz (80g), cheese (preferably low-fat) 4oz (100g), butter 2oz (50g), unsaturated oil (preferably safflower or sunflower) 4fl oz (125ml), extra virgin olive oil 5fl oz (150ml).
Vegetables—potatoes 3½lbs (1.75kg), frozen vegetables 3oz (80g), fresh greens and other vegetables minimum 2½lbs (1.25kg), canned vegetables 10oz (300g).
Meat—lean only from approx. 2lbs (1kg) total weight before trimming, boning, and cooking comprising: red meat and pork total 8oz (225g), bacon/ham 4oz (100g), sausages 1½oz (40g), poultry 10oz (300g), other meat products 4½oz (120g).
Fish—about 12oz (350g) total weight before filleting.
Fruit—over 2lbs (1kg) fresh fruit, canned fruit (preferably low sugar) 2oz (50g), dried fruit and nuts 4oz (100g).
Rice/pasta/noodles—1lb (450g) (preferably wholewheat pasta and brown rice).
Bread—approx. 3lbs (1½kg) total: wholewheat 1¼lbs (over 500g), white 12oz (350g), brown 12oz (350g), other breads 4oz (100g).
Biscuits—not more than 4oz (100g).
Flour—(preferably wholewheat) about 6oz (160g).
Cereals—(breakfast) 8oz (225g).
Cakes/buns/pastry—under 3oz (under 80g).
Pulses—(lentils, peas) 1½oz (40g).
Beverages—½oz (15g) dried.
Sugar—5oz (130g).
Jam/marmalade—4oz (100g).
Other foods—about 9oz (270g).

For vegetarians, omit the fish and meat. Increase pulses, nuts and eggs, low-fat milk and low-fat cheeses to make sure of enough protein. Use soya protein (TVP) and tofu instead of the meat allowance.

Now look at what the problems are when this range and balance of food has to be turned into a non-chew diet:

Milk	No problem, although too much reliance on it as a food can lead to other difficulties. It is prone to mucus-forming in some people.
Eggs	These need to be mashed if hard-boiled, can be soft-scrambled. Poached egg can be chopped, soft-boiled egg gives a problem with the white and fried egg is chewy; omelette is also chewy.
Fats and oils	No problem. Hard cheese can be grated finely but should not be served melted; cottage cheese needs putting through a fine mesh sieve; soft cheeses are inclined to be chewy except for cream cheese; butter and margarine are not a problem if used sparingly. Cream should be used as a treat, not every day.
Vegetables	Potatoes can be mashed after boiling or baking; chips are chewy if crisp, roast potatoes are chewy but soft-centred; fried boiled potatoes can be chopped small; all other vegetables can be cooked and processed/mashed/chopped very finely (see chapter 7), even salads.
Meat	Being fibrous and inclined to dry out after cooking and cooling, most types require processing if tender (ham) or putting through a mincer (raw or cooked beef, lamb, pork, poultry); sausages have chewy skins which need to be avoided; pâté is usually soft if *finely* textured, coarse pâté is too chewy (see chapter 7).
Fish	Bones are a problem; some fish flakes coarsely and needs to be chopped or processed. Canned fish is cooked and can usually be mashed, or if not soft enough (tuna) can be processed; canned salmon and sardines have soft bones which can be mashed.
Fruit, nuts	Fresh fruit is usually chewy except for ripe bananas. It can be processed to a purée, juiced, squeezed or stewed according to type; canned fruit can be processed or sometimes mashed; dried fruit can be processed after soaking and cooking; nuts are a

21

difficulty as they require processing and a further pounding to a paste.

Rice/pasta/ noodles   Rice requires puréeing after cooking as grains are too large not to be chewed, ground rice is a useful ingredient; pasta is by nature a chewy food and requires a special approach (see chapter 4).

Bread   Special soft breads are required which don't need to be chewed; breadcrumbs (homemade) can be used in many ways to use up the amount of bread suggested (see chapter 4).

Biscuits   Although some can be dunked in a hot drink to make them soft, many are unsuitable; some can be made into crumbs and used in recipes. Usually biscuits are high in fat, sugar and salt.

Flour   Can be used for some crumble toppings, sauces and thickenings for gravy, coatings for fish and meat.

Cereals   Many problems with the high fibre (bran) chewy types, no problem with oats. Weetabix goes soft after soaking for five minutes.

Cakes/buns/ pastry   Only soft, specially-made types are suitable; cooked pastry needs to be processed as it is a tough food.

Pulses   Ideal for purées after soaking and cooking.

Beverages   No problem.

Sugar   No problem.

Jam/ marmalade   Only jelly types or specially processed jams and marmalades are suitable (see chapter 14).

Other foods   Confectionery is a problem as chewiness is a typical feature (see chapter 12). Sauces are not a problem; chutney and pickles need to be processed to cope with crisp pieces of vegetable; yoghurt is better homemade to avoid pieces of unchewable fruit and nuts.

All these problem foods are dealt with throughout this book.

BALANCED DIET AND HEALTHY EATING

Basic daily balance of foods for a healthy mixed diet

Type of food	Total amount	Choose from:
high starch	3–4 portions	wholemeal bread, pasta, rice, potatoes, dumplings, pancakes, porridge/cereal, pizza (base).
'greens'	1 portion	green cabbage, spinach, kale, spring greens, dark green lettuce, etc.
vegetables	4 portions	carrots, onions, peas, green beans, leeks, parsnips, turnips, swedes, celeriac, courgettes, peppers, tomatoes, salad vegetables, etc.
fruit	3 portions	apples, oranges, pears, bananas, pineapple, grapes, berry fruits, peaches, apricots, cooking apples, plums, soft fruits, etc.
high protein	2 portions	meat, fish, eggs, low fat cheeses, TVP, beans, tofu, nuts.
fats/oils	2 tablespoons	sunflower oil, extra virgin olive oil, soft margarine, butter.
sugar	1 tablespoon	sugar, jam, honey.
milk	¼ pint (150ml)	milk made with low-fat milk granules (powdered milk) half-fat milk.
treats	1 small portion	biscuit, cake, chocolate, sweets, snacks.

This table only provides a basis—other food/drink is added in the form of flour (as a thickener), herbs and spices, extra high protein and starch, wine, fruit juice, beer, etc. Fats/oils, sugar and treats are extras to avoid and so are salt and salty foods. One desirable extra is wheat bran which can be added to homemade bread and porridge or cereal.

Although it may seem an impossible mountain to climb, a soft options diet only needs application; it certainly isn't difficult. It allows a healthy range of foods to be eaten and enjoyed. The recipes and guidance in this book are designed to help you cope easily with the problem of providing food for people who cannot chew, or have difficulty chewing.

Now for other kinds of food problem which may be cause for health concern and which need to be discussed: the use of gelatine, raw eggs and soft cheeses: BSE, CJD, salmonella and listeria.

Using gelatine

This book is published at a time when CJD, BSE doubts, fears, scares and media dramas fuel the flames of concern. To make some gelatines, all parts of a beef carcass are processed, even the hide. Surely this means a high risk is involved in eating any food that contains gelatine. Alas, nobody really knows yet. A proportion of the population are afraid to eat it. Another proportion couldn't care less about it and the rest don't even think about it. It is used in many processed foods, such as yoghurt, as a thickener and setting agent. Vegetarians and vegans don't eat it on principle; the rest of us probably eat it unknowingly.

For the purposes of this book, only one recipe contains gelatine— old-fashioned homemade jelly. So, if you wish to avoid gelatine, just avoid that particular recipe and take care not to buy unflavoured yoghurt or any other product that contains gelatine.

Using mayonnaise

From time to time hysteria breaks out regarding salmonella and the use of raw eggs. A finger is always pointed at mayonnaise. Commercial firms who manufacture and market mayonnaise don't seem to have a problem with it. How has mayonnaise-eating mankind survived for centuries? Could it be that healthy man is designed to combat such problems? The other side of the coin is the risk to people who are too frail or weak to cope with raw eggs. (How many eggs are infected?) Government warnings are there to be heeded— no raw eggs or raw egg food for the pregnant, ill, elderly or frail. It is possible to make mayonnaise with hard-boiled egg yolks instead of raw and there are other forms of salad dressing that don't involve raw eggs. There is also a type of mayonnaise which is cooked. (See chapter 6 for recipes.)

Cooked eggs

Cooked eggs often have partly cooked yolks—for example, fried, soft-boiled, poached or baked. These are all eggs with runny yolks. Scrambled, hard-boiled and omelette all have completely cooked yolks.

Listeria

The same guidelines are offered for listeria as for salmonella, except that the source is not eggs but soft cheeses and liver pâtés. For health safety they are not recommended for the pregnant, ill, elderly or frail.

Hygiene

Kitchen cleanliness is of prime importance. Regularly clearing out and cleaning the fridge, appropriate storage of food, scrupulously clean equipment and work surfaces, clean hands and nails should be part of your routine. Supermarkets and local councils issue free booklets on the subject. A good standard of hygiene is essential to avoid food poisoning and 'stomach bugs'.

A little of what you fancy ...

Eating whatever you fancy is how most people choose their food. Rarely does it turn out to be a healthy selection. Although a lifetime of eating in this way, with total disregard for health and future well-being, usually results in disaster, there is a great deal of encouragement to follow this style of eating. Cooking programmes on TV, lavish recipe books and magazines and an aggressive attitude to being guided about health and what to eat, don't help. The universal feeling that it doesn't matter what you eat so long as you enjoy it is a matter for despair. However, there are people for whom it is too late to change to a healthier diet-lifestyle. Their undoing then becomes their comfort. (Anyone with a limit on their days should be allowed to eat whatever they feel they would like or can manage. Make sure the food is processed and presented appropriately, however extraordinary it seems. Obviously this goes beyond the concept of caring cuisine and enters the realms of compassionate cuisine.)

Eating comfortably

The most difficult way to eat is from a plate with a knife and fork. A bowl and spoon are easier to manage but there is still quite a long way from the table to the mouth. If the bowl is held near the mouth then the problem is not so great.

People who are fit and able may find a knife and fork unsuitable for some soft options food. A spoon of a size between a teaspoon and a dessert spoon with a matching fork will probably be of most use.

Food that doesn't make it to the mouth will tend to land on clothes, the table and anyone close by. This is vexing for everyone, not just the person eating, and makes for a lot of work clearing up. As well as a small paper napkin close to the mouth, a much larger fabric napkin underneath it will be greatly appreciated. Rarely does one see such large ones on sale but they are easy enough to make. (Seersucker is a good idea as it doesn't need ironing.) Someone who is allowed to get in a mess every mealtime is not really being cared for properly. The result is loss of dignity as well as a lot of cleaning up for the carer.

Some people who have difficulty chewing, require extra liquid with their food. This can be in the form of a sauce, gravy or a drink with the food. Sometimes a glass of water will help, sipped between mouthfuls.

Soft options eaters should be encouraged to savour the non-chew food by holding it in the mouth and moving it around with the tongue if possible. It is important to lubricate the food with saliva which contains enzymes to start off the digestive process. Bolting specially prepared food can still result in indigestion and problems regarding absorption of nutrients.

For people who are disabled and have limited use of their hands there is a variety of specially designed cutlery to help. This can usually be ordered via the pharmacy or chemist, with other aids for the disabled. Getting the right tool for the job is the first step to building skill for easier living. It helps the cared-for and the carer. Anything, however minor, that can be done to help people keep their dignity is never a waste of effort. Every help for disability makes for better ability, which is always positive. It is so easy to give up and be negative. Eating is one of life's pleasures. It may not take the same form as ordinary food but it can still be enjoyed by people with chewing difficulties.

Feeding

There is a knack in feeding someone else with food. It needs to be done at the right pace, with the correct-sized spoonful. The food needs to be put into the person's mouth, not just to the lips, with a large napkin to catch the inevitable spillages. Sitting facing someone to feed him or her is more difficult than at their side. An experienced carer or professional to show you how it is best done would be invaluable. Although only a simple act, feeding someone can be a misery for that person if you get it persistently wrong. The worst offence is to use too large a spoon and to overfill it. The temperature of the food should be appropriate for the person being fed.

If feeding takes a long time due to difficulties, divide hot food into two amounts and keep one half warm while you feed the first half. Ice-cold food is not really appropriate. It should be seen as a novelty or an entertainment. Ice-cream and sorbet are two such foods, often chosen for the non-chewer because basically they are soft—or would be without the ice crystals.

Size of meals
Food which is puréed or finely chopped will go down to about half its original size. Bear this in mind when dishing up, as it is very easy to overestimate a portion and give people far too much. Sometimes it looks better to serve the puréed food in a dish or bowl rather than a plate which may seem inappropriate and over-large.

Remedies
Hiccups—put your index fingers ¼in (6mm) into your ears. Press down for about 7 or 8 seconds. The hiccups should stop.
Sore throat—put 2 teaspoons honey on a tablespoon. Squeeze a few drops of fresh lemon juice on to it. Stir with a teaspoon and swallow slowly. Your sore throat should feel easier.
Indigestion—drink a glass of hot water.

CHAPTER 3

Cooking Equipment and Techniques

As soft options cuisine is concerned with fine chopping rather than just liquidising and blending, it is important to have various items of chopping equipment. Gadgets abound in mail-order catalogues, in kitchen shops and the kitchen departments of stores. I regret to say many of them are a waste of money. Having run the gauntlet of just about every chopper available and wasted a fair amount of money, I eventually ended up using four basic pieces of chopping equipment. They are a board, two knives and an electric 'mini-chopper'.

Chopping
A large chopping knife with a shaped handle and stainless steel blade is definitely required in the soft options kitchen. It is best to go to a specialist shop and actually handle knives to see which one will be best suited to your hand. Don't buy one which feels too heavy as you will be using it a lot.

There is one good habit which will stop you cutting your fingers: always hold the knife so that the blade is angled very slightly away from your fingers as it cuts towards the board. Keep deliberately cutting this way and eventually it will become habit.

Never look away or allow yourself to be distracted when you are cutting up food—it is a serious activity and one in which carelessness can be followed by injury. When chopping round-shaped items such as onions, cut off a little slice to make a flat surface or cut in half. Rest it on this to stop it rolling about while you chop.

Cutting board
All kinds of cutting boards are available—wood, plastic, marble and who knows what. If using a large, sharp chopping knife, a wooden board of pine or oak is comfortable as it accepts the action of the knife blade and avoids slipping. Other, harder woods are probably not as comfortable to use. (Beware of decorative chopping boards which look attractive but are not up to the job.) Marble chopping boards are really only suitable for cheese. Plastic-type 'boards' are useful for cutting items such as garlic and herbs as they are easier to clean. One large board for vegetables and one for bread is probably all you need. Some people prefer to keep a small board specially for chopping herbs. A medium-sized plastic type 'board' for cutting up and chopping hot food would also be useful. Rectangular boards are the ideal shape, although a round wooden board for cutting bread is traditional.

Knife sharpener
A good, simple knife sharpener is essential. This doesn't mean an expensive one, but one you will find easy to use. Again, a specialist shop will allow you a good look at the merchandise. Some people find an old-fashioned steel the easiest to use and perfectionists will enjoy using a whetstone. This can be bought at an ironmongers as it is normally used for sharpening chisels. The sharper your knife, the better it will perform. Always treat it with respect tempered by a little fear. If it comes with a blade protector or sheath, don't throw this away but make a habit of using it (store the knife out of the reach of children).

Mezzaluna and board (optional)
These two are fashionable and so are available. They allow an effective, quick chopping action using two hands, one on each of the round handles, and a curved (concave) board which takes the shape of the curved knife. The mezzaluna can be rocked quickly from side to side or lifted up and brought down sharply to make a

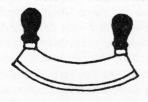

series of long cuts. This type of knife is quite frightening and on no account should it be used with only one hand—if both hands are on the handles you cannot cut yourself. It is useful for cutting up hot food such as potato and for chopping onions, herbs and mushrooms. Keep it sharp and store it with the blade covered.

Mini-chopper

This is an electrical appliance like a miniature food processor. It is basically intended for chopping up food for babies being weaned, so small quantities can be produced. Annoyingly, a full-size food processor is too large and the mini-chopper often too small for soft options adult food. There are several kinds on the market, obtainable from electrical goods shops or kitchen shops. Mail-order catalogues also have them. They are all much of a muchness and I cannot recommend one rather than another.

Mouli

This is an old-fashioned hand mill that is still popular. At first glance it appears to have been invented by a maniac! It comprises a curious-looking holder with a handle, a pierced, removable domed plate with a lot of holes (a choice of three hole sizes), and another handle which hooks on to the holder. This handle can be rotated and its shaped attachment forces the food through the holes into a waiting bowl underneath. The mouli is used for cooked fruit and vegetables. It is a peculiar but effective hand-powered gadget which will make coarse or medium mixtures or fine purées. It fell out of favour somewhat when liquidisers and blenders appeared, yet it produces much thicker purées and coarser mixtures which are soft but not liquid.

The last of the cooked food never goes through the holes and it makes washing up a chore. Wiping with kitchen paper before rinsing under the tap and washing it up properly is the preferred cleaning ritual. Although it looks peculiar it does an excellent job, and often its coarser, soft mixtures are just what are wanted. You will probably only ever need to use the large-holed plate, but it comes with a medium and fine one too.

Stainless steel models are available from food kitchen shops as well as by mail order. Buy the genuine article and not a decorative version because it needs to be very strong. The best ones have foldaway supports underneath. When these are opened the mouli

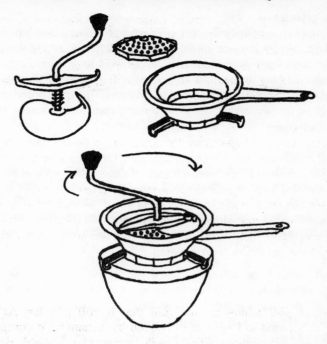

can be supported over saucepan or bowl while the food is processed through.

Liquidiser/blender

This has really become an essential gadget in the kitchen. It comprises a motor to drive a cutting blade at high speed and a goblet. Solid food combined with liquid is pulverised into a completely liquid form. It is useful for most types of soup and for preparing liquids for jelly, desserts, sauces and fruit juice. However, it has its limitations as it will only produce a liquid, whereas a mouli can produce thick purée without any liquid being added. Unless your liquidiser goblet is a heatproof glass one, don't make the mistake of putting into it liquids which are too hot. Although there is a lid, too much liquid will encourage it to splash out when the motor is switched on. The easiest way to clean the blade inside the goblet is to put a cup of hot water into it with a dash of washing-up liquid and switch on for a few seconds. Rinse and leave upside-down to dry. The blade is a dangerous tool: *never* put your fingers inside the goblet while it is operating. Keep it switched off at the wall or unplugged when you are not using it.

Coffee grinder

Usually an extra which will work off the same motor as the liquidiser, the coffee grinder is more useful than it first appears. Being designed to grind rock-hard coffee beans, it takes well to grinding nuts and will reduce bread to crumbs in seconds. It is good policy not to overfill the grinder. It can be cleaned by grinding a little bread which can then be thrown away. Only use for dry items such as nuts, bread and coffee beans.

Mixing bowl

You will need large mixing bowls for bread and cakes, smaller bowls or basins for general mixing and small ones for storing food in the fridge. A set which can be stacked one inside the other will take up the least space. Toughened glass, stainless steel or china can be bought in ironmongers or in kitchen shops or departments.

Grater

A small mouli hand grater is useful for cheese and raw root vegetables for salads. It is rather fiddly to wash up but very effective. A box-shaped hand grater is the alternative. Avoid graters with all kinds of grating cutters which you'll never use. Probably a flat one that can be laid over a basin to catch the gratings will be best.

Wooden spoons

Keep one for savoury cooking, one for anything containing garlic or onion and one for cakes. When they start to get decrepit, throw them away and buy new ones.

Baking tins

Non-stick tins are unnecessary but are probably easier to wash up. Baking sheets for rolls and pastry, sponge tins and patty tins are all you require for soft options cooking. For bread you will need 1lb (½kg), 2lb (1kg) and 3lb (1½kg) loaf tins.

Sieves and strainers

These are often needed. Buy good-quality stainless steel strainers, not plastic. Small, medium and large are useful. If you prefer just one, buy the largest.

Measuring jug

The easiest measures to use for cooking are imperial—pounds and ounces, pints and fluid ounces. The metric gramme is uncomfortably small as a unit of measurement for most people. Older people who have used imperial measures all their lives find it too difficult to change.

Measuring scales
High-tech electric scales may not be as easy to use as the old-fashioned scales with a scale pan and weights. The latter never needs a new battery and is perfectly suitable for any kitchen.

Rolling-pin
A plain wooden rolling-pin is ideal. You will need it for crushing pasta noodles as well as for rolling out pastry.

Whisk
A hand whisk with two beaters is all you need. An improvement on this technically is the electric version, but for instant control the hand whisk has the edge. A wire balloon whisk skilfully wielded might be just as effective, and whichever type you favour it will rarely be used for soft options cooking.

Hand masher
A simple tool for mashing potato, root vegetables and soft fruit is invaluable. The traditional sort with a wooden or plastic handle (rather than all metal) will be easiest to use. It should have a flat plate with holes and a handle positioned over it. When pressed down it compresses the cooked food and forces it up through the holes—puréed.

Mincer
This is a rather old-fashioned tool. It is primarily for mincing meat, cutting through its tough fibres and pushing it out of the machine. A metal one is best. It may need greasing on certain parts to stop it rusting. Keep it in a strong plastic bag with all its bits. After cleaning, dry with a cloth and then put it into the oven after you have finished baking, when it is still warm but switched off. This will dry it completely.

Large food processor
If catering for just one person, a large food processor will be much too large. They basically come in family size and will not handle small amounts. Some are very complicated, will do just about every-thing and are sophisticated electrical gadgets. Often they will do a simple job that is better accomplished by hand with an ordinary

kitchen tool that makes for the minimum of washing up. For large amounts of puréed food and finely grated root vegetables for salads, they are excellent. Meat or fish can be processed to make a soft paste, pulverising it, but not in a small quantity.

Pestle and mortar

There are lots of pretty ones in the kitchen shops made of wood. However, these are really for decoration—they will not stand up to the pounding a good pestle and mortar is designed for. A medium-sized tough ceramic one with a ceramic and wood handle is ideal for pounding herbs and nuts to a paste. Always chop first whatever you are going to pound as this starts the process speedily. Chop nuts as small as you can on a chopping board with a knife, then put into the mortar and pound away. Put through a fine sieve, and any pieces of nut that won't go through the mesh can be put back into the pestle and pounded again.

Spreading knife

A flat rounded blade with a comfortable handle is essential for speed of spreading. It is also more efficient than a pointed knife.

Bread knife

For cutting soft bread you will need a sharp knife with a serrated edge. As bread is quite a large item the knife should be long, with a strong blade. A sawing action is needed, so a knife which has a blade edge resembling a saw-blade is ideal. The handle should feel comfortable to you. A bread knife is used very near your fingers so it is really important to have maximum control.

Kitchen scissors

These are a must in any kitchen. A strong pair will be able to cut up raw fish, meat or herbs and chop up tomatoes in the tin. The best ones come apart for cleaning.

Citrus juicers

There are three types, all of which do the job well. First, a wooden kind to turn round in half a lemon or orange when you require just a small amount of juice quickly. The second kind is a shaped, fluted cone over a shallow bowl. The half fruit is turned backwards and forwards round the cone and the juice runs into the bowl underneath. The third type is really an electric version of the second. Instead of turning the fruit by hand it is held in one position over the cone which is turned for you. Again the juice is caught in a shallow bowl underneath.

Juice extractors/juicers

These are quite powerful gadgets, as well as being fairly large. The fruit and vegetables to be juiced are fed into the machine by hand. The machine shreds them very finely and extracts the juice which collects in a container. The waste pulp collects in a different container and is discarded. Some are more complicated than others. As they need to be taken apart and thoroughly cleaned each time they are used, one which dismantles and can be cleaned easily is a plus. I have yet to find one which runs quietly (some make a quite deafening noise).

Apple corer

This is an extremely simple tool, comprising a handle and a kind of cutting tube. Just turn it into the centre of a cooking apple and the core is pushed away upwards, out of the tube and the apple is left with a neat cavity instead of a core.

Vegetable knife

A small peeling knife is essential. Keep it sharp and be careful not to throw it away by mistake with the peelings. It should feel comfortable and balanced in your hand.

Slotted spoon

This is a large perforated spoon with a long handle. It is ideal for fishing solid food out of liquid. The liquid will drain out of the holes.

Fish slice/spatula

Some flexibility is required so that it can be nudged under fried food without breaking it up. The more expensive ones tend not to be flexible but rather more heavy. A cheap one is perfectly good for the task.

Ladle

This is only a cup on a long handle. It is ideal for spooning soup into bowls or using when you need an extra large spoon for liquid.

Tongs

Metal tongs will save you burning your fingers and dropping hot food.

Oven gloves
The old-fashioned, heavy woven sort with a pocket at each end for the hands are probably the best buy. Many are just something pretty to hang up in the kitchen and do not protect well.

Timer
Essential if you make your own bread; useful if you are baking cakes. One that you can carry with you is preferable to a gadget built in to your stove.

Storage tins
Good-quality tins with tight-fitting lids will keep food better. Small, medium and large sizes are useful—in other words, don't have all one size. Some plastic boxes encourage condensation if stored in the kitchen. However, they are ideal for using in the fridge.

Casseroles
Heavy cast iron casseroles are excellent for slow cooking on the hob or in the oven, but, if they are too heavy for you to lift when full you could have a problem. Consider pottery ones if the weight beats you, or flame-proof ceramic ones.

Saucepans
The passion for sets of saucepans as opposed to odd pans has filled kitchen cupboards with pans that are never used. Just buy what you will need. Non-stick is not the ideal finish for any kind of pan except one for sauce or porridge. Vigorous cleaning will eventually remove the non-stick surface and new pans will need to be purchased. Stainless steel pans are ideal for frequent use. Those with handles that don't heat up are to be cherished but are difficult to come by. Each of your pans should have a lid except the sauce-pan and frying-pan. Sizes can range from a really small pan for boiling an egg to a large one that will take a bag or two of spinach or a lot of water to cook pasta.

Frying-pan and omelette pan
These are really broad-based saucepans with low sides and no lid. Heavy-based ones are most effective.

Gravy separator
This is basically a boat-shaped jug with two spouts. One takes liquid from the top of the jug and the other, liquid from the bottom. See chapter 6 for instructions on how to use it when making gravy.

Automatic breadmakers

Basically, these are miniature, computerised ovens with facilities for mixing, kneading, proving and baking a loaf of bread. Once the ingredients have been put into the appliance and it has been programmed, it needs no more attention. They are expensive—about half the price of a conventional stove—but some people find them a boon. A minority of companies provide a good back-up service with staff to sort out baking problems, but the rest are merely marketing operations to sell as many as possible. These have no back-up in respect of practical advice, should the customer need it. Some of the manuals that arrive with the appliances are badly translated from a foreign language. Others have American weights and measures (although it doesn't say this on the instructions) which are different from those in the UK—for example, the UK pint has 20fl oz, the USA pint has 16. As measurements are critical for automatic breadmakers, this can lead to grief and loaves which go straight into the bin, to say nothing of wasted time and energy.

NOTE: Recipes for bread made by hand cannot be used in an automatic breadmaker without some adjustment. For instance, less yeast is required and a different amount of liquid. This is why a practical consumer service is essential and preferable to sales staff merely trying to sell you a machine. You may need to experiment yourself, using guidance and the advice of skilled operators.

Miscellaneous

Every kitchen should have a jumble of baking dishes, odd simple tools and obscure equipment rarely used. Stainless steel, china or ovenproof glass dishes are available from kitchen shops, departments and mail-order companies. However, beware of buying kitchen equipment which is merely decorative and not strictly functional. Plastic gadgets are often a let-down, particularly if they have cutting edges which are too blunt to use. There seem to be electrical gadgets for many kitchen tasks which are performed more easily by hand but which add considerably to the washing up. Only by practising and improving can skills be gained. Pressing a button requires relatively little effort by contrast.

Good-quality tools and equipment, electrical goods excepted, properly looked after will last a lifetime and be a pleasure to use. (See Appendices for useful addresses.)

COOKING TECHNIQUES FOR SOFT OPTIONS

It is not unusual for troublesome food which cannot be chewed to be left off the menu, quite unnecessarily. Most food can be processed in some way to make it suitable. Here is a selection of problem foods and some idea of solutions. Please don't think these are just fads or ways of placating people who set out to be a nuisance to the cook. For some people with sore gums, even strawberry pips are something to avoid; for others without much jaw movement, even mashed potato can be a problem if it is too stiff in texture. Common sense can go a long way to alleviating such problems.

Sandwiches
See chapter 13 for special soft sandwiches which are made in a different way from ordinary sandwiches.

Pastry
The very nature of pastry is crispness and chewiness—a nightmare food! Bake a piece of pastry, just flat on a baking sheet. Chop it very finely with a large chopping knife, on a board. If something even finer is required, break it into small pieces and make it into crumbs in a coffee grinder. Sprinkle thickly over suitable food such as stewed apple or meat. Make sure there is enough moisture to dampen the crumbs—custard, juice, gravy as appropriate.

Preparing a pie for soft options serving
Cut out the slice you want to serve. Cut away and discard the crust. Take off the pastry lid and put on to a board. With a large chopping knife, chop one way and then the other to make fine crumbs. Spoon the filling on to the serving plate. Cover with the pastry crumbs. Serve with custard, single cream or fruit juice for a fruit pie and gravy for a savoury pie.

If the pie has pastry underneath as well, this too will have to be chopped. Put it on the serving plate and cover with the filling, then proceed as above. The filling too may have to be chopped or processed in a mini-chopper. Add some kind of suitable liquid if it is too dry.

If the pie is a hot one, serve on a warmed plate.

NOTE: It is tempting to chop both pastry and filling in one operation. This results in a very unattractive solution—the quick but unpopular method! See chapter 4 for more information on soft options pastry-making.

Biscuits

Biscuits without a cream filling, or a coating or topping, can be broken into pieces and reduced to crumbs in a coffee grinder. Mixed with soft margarine or butter, these crumbs can be rebaked to form a crumbly textured biscuit pastry. Plain biscuits such as digestives, rich tea, shortbread or ginger nuts will all respond to dunking in tea or coffee to soften them. There is quite an art in dunking as part of the biscuit must be kept dry to act as a handle. If too large a portion is dunked its weight will cause it to fall off into the cup.

Cakes

Even sponge has a crust, albeit a thin one, which some people will find difficulty in eating. See chapter 11 which deals with the crust on cakes. There are also recipes for soft-textured cakes that are easy to eat.

Dried fruit for rich fruit cakes and Christmas puddings

By nature, vine fruits have tough, almost plastic-like skins, extremely chewy and made worse by drying. They must be finely chopped.

Buy good-quality, branded dried fruit that you know will be plump and moist. Inferior quality can be dry, disappointingly hard and tasteless. If you wish to use mixed dried fruit you must remove the tough, rubbery citrus peel. It can be replaced with finely grated orange and lemon rind. Alternatively, mix your own selection of equal amounts of sultanas, seedless raisins and plump currants. Chopped ready-to-eat prunes, and apricots can also be mixed in.

Glacé cherries are a difficult ingredient as they are so tough. Cut in half and remove the soft centres with a coffee spoon or the point of a knife. Chop these on a board, sprinkling with flour to keep the pieces separate. Keep away from the other fruit until you stir them in to the cake or pudding mixture. Dessert grade dates can also be used. Cut out the stones and chop finely on a board, sprinkling with flour to keep the pieces separate.

Salad vegetables

Salads are an enjoyable and important part of the diet. They are well worth attention. See chapter 8, which tells you how to cope with them.

Fruit and vegetables

See chapters 5 (for fruit) and 8 (for vegetables) and the following specific instructions.

Pips and seeds

Strawberry pips

Now that strawberries are available all year round instead of being just a summer treat, they have become more of a difficulty for soft options, appearing more frequently than before. Believe it or not, for some (not all) people, the tiny seeds on the outside of the fruit can lead to problems. Just one embedded in an injured or sore gum, or a few wedged under a dental plate or between teeth and gums, can be excruciatingly painful and lead to infection. For these people strawberries tend to be off the menu. However, it is neither ridiculous nor impossible to serve strawberries without the pips. If it seems wasteful the off-cuts can be used to make juice for someone else who doesn't have this problem.

Choose larger fruit if you can, twice as many as you would normally prepare. Wash the fruit, hull and cut a slice off the top and bottom. Cut what is left into long slices (top to bottom). Lay flat on a board and cut the skin off each side, putting the trimmings well away. Mash the trimmed slices on a plate, using a fork.

Raspberry, blackberry, loganberry pips

Fruit will need to be washed, hulled and mashed on a plate using a fork. Put into a fine mesh sieve over a basin and use the back of a metal spoon to push the pulp through. The pips will be left behind in the sieve.

Preparing tomatoes

The tomato is doubly problematical. First, it has a skin as strong as plastic, and second, it contains flat seeds which seem to have been designed for getting under dental plates.

Spear a tomato with a fork. Hold in a basin of boiling water for a minute. The skin should split. Cool under the cold tap and peel off the skin. Cut into quarters and use a spoon to remove the clusters of pips. The remaining flesh can be finely chopped on a board or puréed in a mini-chopper.

Pasta
See chapter 4.

Chutney and pickle
See chapter 14 for preparation of bought varieties and for soft, trouble-free chutney recipes.

Jam and marmalade
See chapter 14 for ways of dealing with bought varieties and for recipes for making your own.

Steaming
This technique is used for light sponge and soft pastry puddings. It is a slow method of cooking on the hob. The pudding is prepared and put into a basin, covered with a greaseproof paper lid and put into a saucepan of simmering water. This is kept simmering until the pudding is cooked.

The basin
This should be of a kind that will withstand the heat. Heatproof glass and china ones are ideal. There are plastic types, but make sure yours is boil-proof.

Paper lid
This requires a double thickness of greaseproof paper, larger than the circumference of the basin top and large enough to have a pleat across the top, for expansion.

String

Old-fashioned string is best as it needs to withstand the heat. It should be tied under the rim to keep the greaseproof paper on securely and also made into a handle so that the hot pudding can easily be lifted out of the saucepan.

Grid

If you don't have a proper metal grid to put into the bottom of the saucepan, use three metal forks or spoons. The basin should not have direct contact with the bottom of the saucepan.

Saucepan

This has to hold the grid, the steaming water and the basin, so it needs to be large enough. It should have a lid. During the steaming the lid is kept on, leaving a small gap so that some of the steam can escape. On no account clamp the lid on tightly.

Water

The steaming water must not be allowed to get into the basin, nor should it fall below two-thirds of the way up the side of the basin. From time to time it will need topping up with more boiling water from the kettle. This will ensure that the temperature is maintained.

Fan ovens

If using a fan oven, use the Centigrade temperatures given for conventional ovens and deduct 20°. For instance, Gas 6/200°C/400°F would mean 180°C for a fan oven. Reduce baking time by up to one third—e.g. one hour becomes 40 minutes. The easiest way to calculate the time is to divide the number of minutes' cooking time by three and double the answer. 60 minutes ÷ 3 = 20 minutes, multiplied by 2 gives you 40 minutes. Although this seems very easy, there are many types of fan oven and they vary from one brand to another. Some may require 20° less, others may require 18° less. Baking time reductions may also vary. You really need to know your oven well to make the best use of it. The 20°C less is really only a guide, not a hard-and-fast rule.

Colourings

A limited number of natural colourings can be made at home. Spinach juice, beetroot juice and dark berry juice will colour green, pink and purple. Stew a little in water and the colour will run out. Use sparingly. Raspberries can also be used. Mash a couple on a saucer and use the juice. This is ideal for colouring water icing a pretty pink.

Alcohol

Medication for some people also involves a ban on alcohol. This should be borne in mind when cooking as an alcohol ban doesn't only mean abstaining from glasses of wine, beer or spirits. It also includes the small amounts used, for example, in brandy butter and Christmas cake.

Pepper

Pepper ground from a pepper mill can be too coarse for a soft options diet. Either adjust the grinder to fine or buy already finely ground black or white pepper.

Preparation of fish

For advice on buying and preparing fish, see recipes pp. 125–6.

Folding versus mixing

Often food can be ruined by being mixed until it becomes one texture, one colour and one overall taste. This is an insult, tolerated by babies because they know of nothing else, but not by adults who have a huge memory store of tastes, colours and textures. It is usually kinder and more interesting to *fold* different foods together. Process each individual food and put spoonfuls into a bowl or on to a plate. Turn over lightly with a spoon or fork, once, so that they combine here and there but are not all mixed up together.

Presentation

With foods of similar texture, a variation in the shape they take up on the plate can be made by using small bowls or dishes. Press the purée into a bowl, turn upside down on to the plate and shake out. The purée will look compact and neat. Larger shapes are best in the middle of the plate with smaller ones nearer the edge. Cook shops will have all kinds of moulds, but simple ones are the best for ease of turning out the food. *Coeur à la crème* dishes have a delightful heart shape.

Contrasting coloured layers can be pressed into a small soup bowl. These look impressive, rather like a terrine. Small oval dishes can be used and the result cut in slices. Although it only takes a minute or two to do, the attractive slices appear to have taken a lot of time and trouble. Good combinations are carrot, pea and spinach and leek purées, mashed potato and other root vegetables. Broccoli tends not to hold together. (See p. 120 for Vegetable Terrine.)

There is something about purées which some people find unattractive, so any effort to combat this negative reaction is not wasted. A bold garnish is always a good distraction (see p. 196 for Garnishes). Cutting bread into small pieces ready to eat is not recommended for people able to cut up the bread themselves. Crumbs, on the other hand, are always acceptable. For soup serve crumbs in a small bowl on a saucer with a teaspoon.

Both puréed or very finely chopped salad vegetables look appetising served in layers in a glass bowl but need to be served immediately. The same applies to fruit for fruit salad.

Cake decorations can be a problem. For a soft options solution see p. 199.

Building skills

The more simple the tool the more skill can be developed to use it. With a sharp, large-bladed chopping knife it is possible to chop to a purée. With an electric mini-chopper very little skill is required and the process is quicker. Mashing with a potato masher sometimes produces just as good a coarse purée as a mouli. A table fork will often mash perfectly if the food is soft and there is only a small amount.

Foods best processed in a mini-chopper are peas, beans, cabbage, spinach, lettuce, cucumber, watercress and raw root vegetables (finely grated first). A chopping knife is ideal for a purée of peppers which have tough skin and for tomato flesh. Herbs are also best very finely chopped with a knife. Stubborn herbs should be finished off with a pestle and mortar after chopping.

If you are investing in a new large-bladed chopping knife you'll probably need to practise with it to build skill. A piece of green pepper is a good vegetable to start with, also cucumber. First slice it into lengths, then across to form little cubes, and then do quick chopping. Wipe the pieces off the knife blade back onto the board and scrape the rest of the chopped vegetable back into the centre and chop again. Repeat until the vegetable is actually finely puréed.

When I was little, before mini-choppers, food processors and liquidisers were invented, I used to watch my aunts prepare food for my grandmother who couldn't chew. Their only equipment was an old large-bladed knife, which was sharpened on the back doorstep. The knife was used for cutting bread and carving meat as well as chopping food for my grandmother. They managed perfectly well for nearly twenty years on this minimal equipment because they all developed skill with the knife and it was always kept very sharp.

Using other recipe books

An old copy of Mrs Beeton's *Family Cookery* (1920s) is a treasure
trove of 'soft' recipes which use breadcrumbs. Such old-fashioned
books are often thrown out for jumble or surface in second-hand
bookshops for next to nothing. Your existing library of cookbooks
should still be used, but recipes will have to be tailored for non-chew
foods. Sometimes adapted recipes are impossible, or will take too
much time or suffer too much processing to be recognisable. The
fashion for novelty food from far-flung corners of the world can be
used to advantage, as much of the food could be termed 'soft'. It is
a good idea to keep your own scrapbook for recipes you have worked
out: it is very easy to forget if you don't write them down. There
is no need to be slavish over method if this is obvious—just write
down the ingredients, oven settings and baking time. It will be your
own very personal record of special recipes, nothing like a published
cookbook. So long as *you* can read your own writing, it doesn't
matter if nobody else can!

Ask friends if they will let you look through their collection of
cookbooks to find recipes, or go to the local reference library and
study their collection. Even if there are no specific non-chew recipes
there are bound to be some which you could probably use with a
little imagination.

SAFETY

No wonder there are accidents waiting to happen in kitchens. An
array of sharp tools, electrical gadgets, boiling water, flames, heat,
boiling-hot fat—all manner of dangers are on hand. Here are a few
tips to save cut fingers and burns.

1 Never put a sharp knife into a bowl of water and leave it to
  become obscured by other things put into the bowl for washing
  up. Wash, dry and put the knife away separately and safely.
2 Always use oven gloves as a good habit.
3 If a pan catches fire, don't move it. Turn off the heat under it,
  then cover with a tea towel wrung out in water. Leave it on for
  a long time, until the pan has cooled down. Whatever you do,
  don't throw a bowl of water over the pan as it will not put out
  the flames but rather increase the problem.
4 Don't use pans which are too small for the amount of food cooking
  in them.

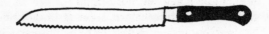

CHAPTER 4

Bread and Basics

Here are the basic staples for soft options cuisine—good soft breads, pastas, pastry, dumplings and pancakes. Although the soft bread section may seem a little too generous, what else will replace biscuits, cakes, crispbreads, cookies, chocolate bars, snacks, sweets and other chewy foods? There has to be something enviable to fill the vacuum. A piece of homemade soft bread and butter is hard to beat—a simple pleasure but an absolute delight.

BREAD

The fact that ordinary commercial bread may not be suitable is no bad thing, since for soft options something far superior is possible. Few of us today are fortunate enough to be able to buy bread from a small bakery which bakes fresh bread daily. Plant bakeries produce most of the bread sold in supermarkets and shops, where the majority of us have to do our shopping. Plant bakery bread is made using an entirely different process from homemade bread, as you would expect. The results are more concerned with price, long shelf-life, how much water the loaves will hold and speed of manufacture, than with flavour, texture and nutrition. Texture is cake-like and mysterious 'improvers', additives and a great deal of salt feature in the ingredients. The shop shelves sag with bread that is several days old. Instore bakeries use part-baked bread made off the premises to re-bake and put on the shelves. The cheapest ingredients are used wherever possible to keep production costs down. This is bad news for 'the staff of life' and even worse news for the people condemned to eat it. Many people have never eaten really good bread in their whole lives, which is a sorry state of affairs.

Good bread, homemade or otherwise, can be a daily pleasure. It is not difficult to make and is well worth the effort, especially when special bread is required as in the case of soft food. Although most plant-baked bread appears to be soft it can be quite tough to eat, requiring a lot of effort to chew. It usually goes stale quickly once the wrapper is opened, which is why toast is so popular—the best way to use it up! There is also the practice of freezing bread, reducing the quality even further.

At home, where there is great flexibility, special breads can be baked to suit soft cuisine. Crustiness is not a prized feature as crusts will be cut off, but a soft texture and maximum nutritional value are all characteristics which can better replace the low price, long shelf-life, speedy manufacture and ability to travel well of commercial bread.

There is a wide choice of flours, yeast, and baking tins and they are not expensive. In spite of the disappointing bread available in shops, bread is still a staple food. The average loaf is most likely to be made from wheat, the cheapest grain, but there are other flours available for variety in breadmaking, for example rye, barley, wheatgerm, soya and so on.

Loaves and rolls

All the recipes that follow are for special soft-textured bread. They have been created specially for soft cuisine and will be new to you, even if you have been baking bread for years.

Medium-sized loaves are preferable to large ones for ease of cutting the soft slices. If you have not filled your baking tins with too much dough you should get a flat-topped loaf. Rolls bake more quickly than loaves but only the centre slice can be used. However, rolls shouldn't be dismissed as unsuitable as the top and bottom crusts can easily be cut off. With some of the modern instant/Easyblend yeasts it is possible to make a few rolls in under the hour. For many of us this can be quicker than trekking to the shops to buy bread.

The aroma of fresh bread baking in the kitchen is irresistible, both pleasurable and anticipatory. Please don't just cave in and buy shop bread if homebaked bread is new to you. Every other day or three times per week will establish the routine to give you a constant supply of a wonderful food. If you have not made bread before, the next few pages

SOFT OPTIONS

are for you. Experienced breadmakers will be familiar with the art and can probably proceed straight to the recipes. However, please heed the advice on filling tins and scan the ingredients list.

BREADMAKING AT HOME

Beginners take heart! Making your own loaves and rolls is not difficult and the rewards are obvious. Several varieties of soft bread can be enjoyed by using a limited selection of ingredients. Here are a few pearls of wisdom about the baking of bread which might be of help to the novice.

Yeast

Don't be frightened of yeast. If you've never used it before you need to understand this magical ingredient. Without yeast, bread is as heavy as a brick and extremely difficult to chew, yet only a small amount of yeast is required to lighten the largest loaf. Yeast is basically a minute fungus which can act on sugar to make carbon dioxide (gas). This is trapped in small bubbles inside the warm bread dough as it rises, and the heat of the oven causes the gas to expand, making the bread rise even more. Continued heat hardens the outside of the bubbles so that the bread holds its risen shape. All the bubbles are trapped in the cooked bread, as the yeast dries when it reaches a temperature of 55°C or 130°F.

Several kinds and brands of yeast are widely available from supermarkets, grocers, health food shops and small bakeries. The type of yeast needed for bread-baking is *baker's yeast*. This is a live, active kind of yeast, quite different from brewer's yeast which is a kind of tonic and a by-product of the brewing industry.

Instant or Easyblend yeast

This is sold in ¼oz (7g) or ½oz (15g) foil sachets and is the easiest type to use and store. (Ignore instructions which indicate only one rising is required. This does not give the dough a chance to 'ripen' and makes for rather indigestible, heavy bread.) The great advantage of this yeast is that it can be mixed straight into flour without being left to work in water and sugar.

Compressed or fresh yeast

This is a dark pinkish-beige colour, sold cut from a soft block. It will keep in the fridge (wrapped) for several weeks and can be kept frozen for months. It needs to be crumbled into a small basin, half

48

full of warm water, and fed with a little sugar (about 1 teaspoon). Left in a warm place, the yeast will start to 'work' and the liquid will become frothy and full of bubbles. After a stir it can be added to the flour. Makes excellent bread but it takes longer than the instant/Easyblend.

Dried active yeast
These dried yeast granules are twice as strong as compressed or fresh yeast—if your recipe says 1oz (25g) then you need only use ½oz (15g). Get it going by sprinkling into warm water with a teaspoon of sugar. Give it a stir after five minutes, then wait until the top is frothy. It takes longer to work than fresh yeast and has a strong, yeasty smell. Use only when the mixture is frothy and not before or your bread will not rise. Can be bought in small tins, or in sachets which should be kept in the dark to avoid deterioration. Firmly close the tin each time you use it. One advantage of this kind of yeast is the lower price; however, some people find it difficult and slow to use. Putting too much yeast into bread will not make it rise more quickly or give you larger loaves, it will merely taste unpleasant. The trick is to put in just enough. Extra yeast ruins the flavour of bread so always put in the amount stated in the recipe.

Warm water
Water that is too hot will kill the yeast. If it is too cool everything will take much longer. One part hot water to two parts cold will give you the correct lukewarm water.

Mixing bowl
As bread dough easily doubles in size you will need a large mixing bowl. A glass or earthenware one is ideal. Lightly oiling the bowl before use will prevent build-up of dough which has to be removed with a knife. When the bowl has been used, soak it in cold water, as opposed to hot. The heat of the water starts to cook the dough which expands, making twice the work.

BREADMAKING TERMS AND PROCEDURES

Kneading
If you are able to watch someone kneading dough, so much the better. If you can have a try yourself, better still. You will need to get used to handling dough and knowing when to stop kneading to let it prove. Here are some hints.

1 Don't knead dough on a cold surface such as slate or marble. A wooden board, table-top or work surface are all ideal. Bread dough likes to be kept warm; that is why warm hands are ideal for kneading it.

2 Flour your hands and the work surface before you begin. Tip the dough out of the bowl, scraping out any left behind. Make a heap of the dough, including any odd bits and pieces. Press it together to make one lump. Flour your hands again. You are now ready to start kneading.

3 Pat the dough flat, then fold half towards you to make a double thickness. Press quite hard with the heel of your hand, down and forward. Use the weight of your body from the waist up and try to be relaxed. Turn the dough round a little, fold again and repeat the action, using one or both hands. Use more flour to avoid the dough becoming sticky and continue to flour the work surface if required. Keep turning the dough until you have gone full circle.

4 When the dough feels smooth and elastic and begins to look a little shiny, fold it over for the last time and place in a large, lightly oiled bowl. Cover with food film and then a clean tea towel. Leave to prove in a warm place (this is called the first rising or proving).

Proving
This means leaving the dough to rise. It needs an even, all-round warmth (not heat!), not just from one direction or the dough will rise unevenly. Depending on the time of year, you can use a sunny windowsill, the airing cupboard, or a shelf or worktop near the stove. Wherever it is, make sure it isn't in a draught as this will slow down progress. In hot summer weather room temperature is enough to prove dough.

Overproving occurs when the dough is left to rise for too long. It goes spongy and will become adventurous, puffing itself over the sides of the bowl and travelling over the work surface. This is probably what frightens people about yeast. There is a science-fiction quality about its behaviour when out of control! If this happens, don't worry. Flour your hands and collect up all the errant bits. Put back into the bowl with the dough still left there and just knead again. It will probably rise more quickly this time, so keep an eye on it after the first 10–15 minutes.

Knocking back
After the first proving, when the dough has doubled in size, it will appear puffy and aerated. Poke it in several places with the handle

50

of a wooden spoon or your finger and it will collapse down into the bowl. The dough is now ready for kneading again.

Slapping down

This would be better described as 'thumping'. It is impressive to watch as well as therapeutic! First flour the worktop. Turn out the dough from the bowl. Flour your hands well and pick up the lump of dough, raise it quickly in the air and thump it noisily down onto the worktop. Do this twice more. The yeast in the dough will be activated to grow vigorously. This simple procedure will save you several minutes of kneading.

Filling tins

Bread has its last rising or proving in the tin or on the baking sheet. Once it has been placed appropriately it mustn't be moved again until after baking. Grease tins well with margarine to ensure bread turns out easily after baking. After the first rising, slapping down and kneading, cut the dough into pieces with a knife. Knead each piece for a minute to shape it to the tin as far as possible. Put into prepared tins, pressing with your knuckles to push the dough into the corners. As soft options bread will need to have all crusts cut off, a flat top to the loaves is less wasteful than a curved one. The way to achieve a flat top is to fill the tins slightly less than halfway up with the unrisen dough. After proving it should not reach the top of the tin. Flour the tops before proving and cover with food film or a clean tea towel. Usually the second rising is much quicker than the first as the dough is in smaller amounts. Leave in a warm place to prove and check after 15 or 20 minutes to see how it is doing.

Finishing loaves

If you are making different kinds of bread at the same time as soft options loaves, mark the latter for identification by snipping the top with scissors in a pattern, before the final rising. Toppings such as sesame seeds, cracked wheat and poppy seeds are inappropriate for soft options as the crusts are always removed.

Baking

Bread is similar to sponge—it doesn't like the oven door opened for the first 15 minutes or it may decide to sink. The oven needs to be hot when the bread is put in or the dough will go on and on rising and become spongy and weak. Rolls are baked on the top shelf, loaves lower down on the centre shelf.

Rolls

If making rolls, have ready a greased and floured baking sheet. After the first rising, slapping down and kneading, shape the dough into a large sausage. Cut off equally-sized pieces with a knife. Knead each one and shape into a ball. Put on to the baking sheet. Flatten with your hands. Leave space around each one as they will expand. Prove until doubled in size and bake for about 12–15 minutes at the top of the pre-heated oven, Gas 7/220°C/425°F. (Don't worry about them being crusty as the top and bottom can be cut off, leaving a slice of round, soft bread. Cut off the crust or use a tumbler to cut out the round of bread.) Cool on a wire rack. use within a few hours of baking. Crusts will be useful for breadcrumbs and should not be wasted.

Baked loaves

If you have greased your tins properly the loaves will just fall out after baking. If by any chance one does stick, bang the bottom of the tin on the worktop to dislodge the loaf. Failing that, run a knife all the way round between the loaf and the tin. At all events, get the loaf out of the tin as quickly as possible or it will start to go wet and soggy. Cool on a wire rack. To see if a loaf is baked, turn it upside down and tap the bottom with your knuckles. A hollow sound means it is indeed done; a dull, thudding sound means it isn't and must go back into the oven to finish baking (no need to put it back in the tin). Bake for a few more minutes, then cool on a wire rack.

Storage

Don't attempt to put loaves in the breadbin until they have completely cooled down (this can take hours). If you wish, wrap in a clean tea towel to prevent drying out, ensuring the bread keeps soft, but if you will be using it quickly just store in the bin unwrapped. Rolls will go stale in a few hours and should only be kept to make into crumbs.

INGREDIENTS FOR SOFT OPTIONS BREAD

Flours

Barley flour—a finely ground, creamy-coloured flour which helps to give a soft texture and a good flavour.
Plain white flour—use unbleached if you can as it has more flavour

than the bleached kind. Quite good on its own but not really strong enough for blends.

Strong white bread flour—this has added wheat protein for a better performance. It will make a strong but light loaf. Too tough on its own but perfect for the basis of various soft options blends.

Rye flour—a greyish, finely ground flour that makes a good keeping bread. It is far too tough used on its own and takes ages to rise but can be used in a blend. Its slightly musty taste doesn't survive baking.

Soya flour—made from beans, this fine yellow flour is used as an addition to a blend as it has a good protein content. It has a slightly musty smell which lessens on baking.

Wholemeal (100 per cent) flour—this is made from whole wheat grains including husks and has three times more fibre than white flour. Organically grown seems to have the best 'nutty' flavour. Brown flour at its commercial best.

Strong brown bread flour—this has added wheat protein to produce bread which is light. Organically grown is best for flavour.

Stoneground brown flour—old-fashioned, properly milled between stones. The healthiest of flours if organically grown wheat is used.

Other ingredients for bread

Bran—made from the tough outer casing of wheat grains. Probably the best addition to the diet to prevent constipation. Will take up plenty of water which makes it swell and soften.

Rolled oats—these are preferable to oatmeal which tends to be tough. Grind in a coffee grinder to make a soft powder to avoid a chewy texture.

Wheatgerm—this is made from the centre of the wheat grains and is highly nutritious. An excellent ingredient in many respects. It is dark gold in colour and can improve the flavour of bread as well as nutritional quality.

Dried milk—use low-fat grade. Helps to produce soft, light bread with a good flavour. Can either be added in dry form to flour or reconstituted as milk.

Malt extract—an extremely thick, sticky substance made from barley. As granary flour is unsuitable for soft options bread due to the hard, malted grains, using malt can give you the flavour without the unwanted texture. It is only added in small amounts and has the advantage of making yeast act faster.

Black treacle—this is the demon version of treacle. It has a high iron content and a strong flavour. It is used in dark-coloured breads.

Only a small amount should be used as it has an intense flavour.

Honey—easiest to use is the runny type as it can be drizzled into dough from a spoon. If using the thick type, mix with a little warm water to soften and thin it down. A sweetener to be used in small amounts.

Salt—use ordinary table salt.

Sugar—caster sugar is ideal.

Eggs—organic, free range are the best. If you can't get organic, just free range is next best.

Olive oil—use extra virgin olive oil which is made from the first pressing of the olives. It tends to toughen bread texture so should only be used in small amounts as a flavouring.

Sunflower oil—a light cooking oil which helps to soften texture and prevent staling. The flavour is bland and unobtrusive.

Shopping
The following are most likely to be available at health food shops: barley, rye and soya flours; extract of malt, wheatgerm, wheat bran; stoneground and organically grown flours. Other ingredients should be available at supermarkets.

BREAD RECIPES

Soft Wholewheat Bread (makes 2 small loaves)
Although soft, these loaves keep well. A simple, healthy brown bread.

½oz (15g) instant/Easyblend yeast	1 tablespoon sugar
3oz (80g) barley flour	½ teaspoon salt
1lb (450g) stoneground wholewheat (strong) bread flour	1 tablespoon oil (extra virgin olive oil, or sunflower oil)
1 heaped tablespoon low-fat dried milk granules	1 egg, beaten
	just under ¾pt (450ml) warm water

Preheat oven: Gas 5/190°C/375°F. *Position*: above centre shelf. *Baking time*: about 30 minutes.

Method: Put the yeast, barley and wholewheat flours, dried milk, sugar and salt into a large bowl. Mix well. Drizzle in the oil then pour in the egg. Mix with a wooden spoon. Pour in the water and stir to a soft dough. Cover with food film and leave to rise in a warm place for about an hour or until spongy and doubled in size. Knock back and turn out on to a floured worktop. Slap down and knead for 3 or 4 minutes. Divide into two. Shape the dough to fit the 1lb (½kg) greased loaf tins. Cover with food film and leave to rise in a warm place until almost to the top of the tins. Bake. Turn out on to a wire rack to cool.

NOTE: The texture of this bread is extra soft and light, which makes it good for slices and crumbles but rather wasteful for sandwiches. However, as such a large proportion of the flour is wholewheat it rather depends on the brand: there will be a difference with each harvest. If an all-purpose bread is required, i.e. for sandwiches, use 12oz (350g) wholewheat flour and 4oz (100g) strong white bread flour instead of 1lb (450g) wholewheat.

Soft Rye Bread (makes 1 long loaf)
Rye flour on its own makes a heavy, leathery-textured loaf that would thwart a crocodile! By adding other flours a softer bread is obtained but still with the distinctive rye flavour. The rye flour is inclined to make the yeast rather lazy so it requires three risings instead of the usual two.

6oz (160g) rye flour
6oz (160g) strong wholewheat
  bread flour
6oz (160g) strong white bread
  flour
½ teaspoon salt
1 tablespoon low-fat dried milk
  granules

¼oz (7g) instant/Easyblend yeast
1 tablespoon extra virgin olive
  oil
1 tablespoon sunflower oil
1 tablespoon black treacle
abut ¾pt (450ml) warm water

Preheat oven: Gas 7/220°C/425°F. *Position*: above centre shelf. *Baking time*: about 35 minutes.

Method: Put the three flours into a large warmed mixing bowl with the salt, dried milk and yeast. Mix well by hand. Drizzle in the two oils and treacle. Mix with a wooden spoon and add enough water to make a heavy, sticky dough. Sprinkle the dough with more wholewheat flour and cover with food film. Leave in a warm place to rise for an hour. (Don't expect too much of a rise at this stage.) Turn out on to a floured worktop and knead, using more flour if required. After 3 or 4 minutes the dough should feel smooth and elastic. Put back into the bowl and cover with food film again. Leave to rise in a warm place for the second time. After 1½ —2 hours it will have doubled in size. Knock back and turn out again on to a floured worktop. Knead well for 2 minutes, slapping the dough down once. Have ready a greased 3lb (1½kg) long loaf tin. Shape the dough to the tin and press into the corners with your knuckles. Sprinkle the top with a little rye flour and leave to rise in a warm place covered with a clean tea towel, for about 30 minutes or so until doubled in size. Bake, turning the heat down to Gas 5/190°C/375°F after 15 minutes. Turn out on to a wire rack to cool.

TIP: A quick way to warm the bowl is to wash it in hot water and dry quickly with a clean tea towel.

Soft Rye Bread with Caraway

Traditionally caraway seeds are sprinkled on the top of rye bread. Since the crusts are cut off for soft options food they will not be eaten. However, they will impart the flavour of caraway. Before the last rising, brush the top of the loaf with milk and scatter with a few caraway seeds. Prick the top in a few places with a fork before scattering on the seeds to let the flavour into the loaf for a stronger taste. After the loaf has baked, take a knife and scrape off all the seeds. This way you will avoid them getting into the bread by mistake.

Soft Half-and-Half Bread (makes 2 × 1lb (½kg) loaves and 6 rolls)

The white flour lightens this bread considerably and the malt extract sets the yeast rising at a cracking pace.

12oz (350g) wholewheat plain flour	½oz (15g) instant/Easyblend yeast
12oz (350g) strong white bread flour	½ teaspoon salt
1oz (25g) wheatgerm or fine oat flour*	1 generous tablespoon malt extract
1 tablespoon low-fat dried milk granules	2 tablespoons sunflower oil
	just under 1pt (600ml) warm water

Preheat oven: Gas 7/220°C/425°F. *Position*: above centre shelf. *Baking time*: 35 to 40 minutes for loaves, 12–15 minutes for rolls.

Method: Put both flours and wheatgerm or oat flour into a mixing bowl with the dried milk, the yeast and salt. Mix well. Drizzle in the malt and oil. Stir in. Make a well in the centre and pour in most of the water. Mix with a wooden spoon, adding a little more water

* Make in a coffee grinder from rolled oats.

56

to make a soft dough. Cover with food film and leave for 30–40
minutes in a warm place or until doubled in size and spongy. Knock
back and turn out on to a floured worktop. Slap down and knead
for 2 or 3 minutes or until dough feels smooth and elastic.

Cut into three equally-sized pieces. Shape two pieces to fit 2 ×
1lb (½kg) greased loaf tins. Press the dough into the corners with
your knuckles. Make the remaining dough into a long sausage shape
and cut into 6 pieces for the rolls. Knead and shape each one, using
more flour. Place well apart on a greased baking sheet. Leave both
loaves and rolls to rise in a warm place, the loaves covered with a
clean tea towel and the rolls uncovered, for about 20–30 minutes
or until doubled in size. Bake rolls on the top shelf and the loaves
underneath. After 15 minutes lower the heat to Gas 5/190°C/375°F
for the loaves. Turn out of tins or take off the baking sheet and cool
on a wire rack.

NOTE: If you don't want rolls, make another small loaf instead.

Soft Oat Bread (makes 3 small loaves)
Moist brown bread with a thin crust that keeps well if wrapped in
greaseproof paper. Although the dough has quite a heavy feel it
rises and bakes quickly.

just less than ¾pt (450ml) water	6oz (160g) rolled oats
1 heaped tablespoon low-fat dried milk granules	2oz (50g) plain white flour
	¼ teaspoon salt
1oz (25g) soft margarine or butter	½oz (15g) instant/Easyblend yeast
12oz (350g) strong wholewheat flour	2 teaspoons sugar
	2 teaspoons sunflower oil

Preheat oven: Gas 6/200°C/400°F. *Position*: above centre shelf.
Baking time: about 30 minutes.

Method: Put the water and dried milk into a small saucepan. Add
the margarine and heat gently, while you stir, until the margarine
has melted. Put aside to cool to lukewarm. Grind the rolled oats in
a coffee grinder to make a soft flour. Grease a large mixing bowl.
Put in the oat flour, brown and white flours, salt, yeast and sugar.
Mix well to combine. Drizzle in the oil, stir and make a well in the
centre. Pour in the lukewarm milk mixture and mix to a soft dough,
adding either a little warm water or more flour, as necessary. Turn
out on to a floured worktop and knead for 3 or 4 minutes, until it
feels smooth. Put the dough back into the bowl and leave to rise in

a warm place, covered in food film. (This should not take more than 30 minutes.)

When doubled in size, knead again for 3 to 4 minutes. Divide equally into three pieces. Grease 3 × 1lb (½kg) loaf tins. Shape the dough to fit the tins, pressing with your knuckles to fill the corners and leaving a slight depression in the centre to ensure a flat top. Cover with food film and leave to rise in a warm place for about 15 to 20 minutes. When doubled in size bake for 10 minutes then turn down the heat to Gas 5/190°C/375°F for a further 15 minutes. Turn out on to a wire rack to cool.

NOTE: It is important to allow the milk mix to cool down to lukewarm before using to mix into the flour. Liquid that is too hot will kill the yeast and the dough will not rise properly.

Soft Malted Bread (makes 1 medium loaf)

1lb (450g) strong white bread flour	3 tablespoons sunflower oil
¼oz (7g) instant/Easyblend yeast	2 generous teaspoons malt extract
½ teaspoon salt	about ½pt (300ml) warm water
2 heaped tablespoons low-fat dried milk granules	more flour for kneading/dusting

Preheat oven: Gas 6/200°C/400°F. *Position*: above centre shelf. *Baking time*: 35–40 minutes.

Method: Warm a large bowl. Put in the flour, yeast, salt and dried milk. Mix well and spoon in the oil. Stir with a wooden spoon to distribute. Drizzle in the malt in a circle, as best you can using 2 teaspoons (it is a thick, sticky ingredient). Pour in just over ½ pint (300ml) warm water and mix again with a wooden spoon. You should have a sticky, wet dough. Sprinkle the top liberally with flour, cover with food film and a clean tea towel; leave to rise in a warm place until doubled in size. Knock back and turn out on to a well floured worktop.

Put a 2lb (1kg) loaf tin to warm while you knead the dough for 4 to 5 minutes, adding more flour. It should be smooth and much reduced in size. Grease and flour the warmed tin and shape the dough into a large sausage. Put into the tin and press into the corners with your knuckles. Leave to rise in a warm place, uncovered, for about 20 minutes or until well risen. Bake. Turn out on to a wire rack to cool. Makes delicately malt-flavoured bread but without the hard malted grains of granary flour, known in the trade as 'the dentist's friend'.

58

The loaf is moist and will keep soft for 2—3 days. A rustic-looking bread of surprising elegance.

Soft Brown Bread (makes 2 medium loaves and 4 rolls)

1lb (450g) strong white bread flour	1 teaspoon salt
2oz (50g) wheatgerm	½oz (15g) instant/Easyblend yeast
4oz (100g) barley flour	1 teaspoon (warmed) black treacle
10oz (300g) wholewheat flour	
1 heaped tablespoon low-fat dried milk granules	2oz (50g) soft margarine
	about 1¼pt (700ml) warm water

Preheat oven: Gas 7/220°C/425°F. *Position*: rolls top shelf, loaves centre shelf. *Baking time*: rolls 12—15 minutes, loaves 30—35 minutes.

Method: Combine all dry ingredients in a large bowl. Drizzle in the black treacle. Mix well and rub in the margarine. Make a well in the centre and pour in the water. Mix with a wooden spoon to make a soft, sticky dough. Cover with food film and leave to prove in a warm place. When doubled in size and spongy in appearance, knock down. Use more flour to slap down and knead until smooth and elastic. Grease 2 × 2lb (1kg) loaf tins. Cut the dough in half. With a floured knife cut enough off each of the two pieces to make two rolls. Shape each large piece of dough to fit the tins, pressing with your knuckles to fill the corners. Grease a baking sheet. Shape four rolls and place on the baking sheet, leaving enough space around each one for expansion. Leave to rise in a warm place.

The rolls will be ready quickly. When doubled in size, soft and puffy-looking, they are ready to bake. Immediately they are baked, put on a wire rack to cool. Turn down heat to Gas 6/200°C/400°F. When the dough in the tins has doubled in size, bake. Turn out of tins on to a wire rack to cool. Use the rolls as soon as possible, cutting off top and bottom and just using the centre slice as round bread, two slices per roll.

Golden Harvest Soft Bread (makes 2 small or 1 medium-sized loaf)

An extremely nourishing multi-grain loaf for people who are not eating well. Although the crust is crisp, the inside is soft-textured. Keeps well and is enriched with extra protein from soya, wheatgerm, egg and milk. It has a fairly heavy texture for kneading but the resulting loaf is light and a golden colour.

8oz (225g) strong white flour
1oz (25g) rye flour
1oz (25g) barley flour
1oz (25g) soya flour
2oz (50g) wholewheat flour
1oz (25g) wheatgerm
1 heaped tablespoon low-fat
  dried milk granules

½ teaspoon salt
2 teaspoons brown sugar
¼oz (7g) instant/Easyblend yeast
1 generous tablespoon malt
  extract
2 tablespoons sunflower oil
1 egg, beaten
about ½pt (300ml) warm water

Preheat oven: Gas 5/190°C/375°F. *Position*: above centre shelf.
Baking time: 25–30 minutes for small loaves or 30–40 minutes for a medium loaf.

Method: Put the five flours into a large bowl. Sprinkle in the wheatgerm, dried milk, salt, sugar and yeast. Mix well by hand to combine evenly. Put in the oil and malt extract. Mix with a wooden spoon. Add the egg and most of the water. Mix again to form a soft dough, adding more water if required. Cover the bowl with food film and leave to rise in a warm place for an hour, until increased in size by half as much again. Flour the worktop and turn out the dough on to it. Knead for 5 minutes adding more flour. Grease a 2lb (1kg) or 2 × 1lb (½kg) loaf tins. Shape the dough to fit the tin(s), pressing with your knuckles to fill the corners. Leave to rise in a warm place, covered with food film. Bake when almost doubled in size. (More rising will take place during baking.) Turn out on to a wire rack to cool.

NOTE: You may find it easier to use a rolling-pin to roll out the dough thickly into a rectangle and then roll it up like a Swiss roll before putting it into the tin(s). If using this method, be sure to roll it firmly, pinching the ends together to prevent holes forming inside the bread.

Soft White Loaf (makes 1 medium loaf)
We are all brought up to know that brown bread is healthier than white, but brown is unsuitable for some people. Here's a white loaf that knocks spots off white shop bread. It makes wonderful golden toast to make into crumbs—all the taste without the chewing.

12oz (350g) strong white bread
  flour
½ teaspoon salt
¼oz (7g) instant/Easyblend yeast
½ teaspoon sugar

1 heaped tablespoon low-fat
  dried milk granules
1 egg, beaten
¼pt (150ml) warm water
2oz (50g) soft margarine, melted

Preheat oven: Gas 8/230°C/450°F. *Position*: above centre shelf.
Baking time: 30—35 minutes.

Method: Put the flour, salt, yeast, sugar and dried milk into a bowl.
Mix to combine. Make a well in the centre and pour in the beaten
egg. Stir, adding the water. Mix really well and turn out on to a
floured worktop. Knead, adding more flour and the melted margarine.
Shape the dough into a ball and put into a warm, slightly oiled bowl.
Cover with food film and leave to rise in a warm place for 30
minutes. Knock back, slap down and knead, using more flour. When
the dough feels elastic and smooth, shape into a fat sausage and
press into a 2lb (1kg) greased loaf tin. Cover with food film and
leave to rise in a warm place for 30—40 minutes until doubled in
size. Bake then turn out on to a wire rack to cool. Keeps fresh for
2—3 days.

Quick Soft Multi-grain Bread (makes 2 medium loaves, or 1
medium plus 1 small and 6 rolls)
No need to get the scales out for this bread—just use 2 spoons.

1 really heaped tablespoon wheat bran

1 really heaped tablespoon wheatgerm

1 really heaped tablespoon low-fat dried milk granules

2 really heaped tablespoons barley flour

2 really heaped tablespoons rye flour

4 really heaped tablespoons strong wholewheat brown bread flour

5 really heaped tablespoons strong white bread flour

3 tablespoons sunflower oil

½oz (15g) sachet instant/Easy-blend yeast

2 teaspoons salt

1 slightly heaped teaspoon sugar

about 10fl oz + (300ml +) warm water

Preheat oven: Gas 6/200°C/400°F. *Position*: centre shelf. *Baking
time*: about 35—40 minutes.

Method: Spoon the bran, wheatgerm, barley and rye flours,
wholewheat and white flour into a large mixing bowl. Add the yeast,
salt and sugar. Mix well and spoon in the oil. Stir well to distribute.
Add enough warm water to mix to a soft dough. Sprinkle with a
little more flour and cover with food film. Put in a warm place to
prove. When doubled in size knock back and turn out on to a floured
worktop. Slap down and knead for 3 minutes. When the dough is
smooth and elastic, divide in half. Shape to fit two 2lb (1kg) greased

loaf tins. Cover with food film and leave to rise in a warm place. When doubled in size, bake. Turn out and cool on a wire rack.

If making rolls, cut off small pieces of dough, roll into shape, flatten and put on to a greased baking sheet. Leave to rise, uncovered, for about 20 minutes or until doubled in size. Bake on the top shelf of a preheated oven Gas 7/220°C/425°F for about 12–15 minutes. Cool on a wire rack.

For Teabread see chapter 11.

PASTA

Commercial pasta is made from hard durum wheat, ground into semolina. This ensures it is strong and will hold its shape while drying. It can then be stored for months or even years until required. After cooking in boiling water for twenty minutes or so it will rehydrate and become soft but still chewy. Cooking it beyond this point will make it slippery and unpleasant in the mouth, so it is served *al dente*, meaning 'to the tooth'. (This means cooked but still slightly firm and a little chewy.) This is not much comfort for people who cannot chew. However, there are several ways of tackling the problem so that pasta can be enjoyed with its rich variety of sauces, although bear in mind that overcooking to soften the pasta is not the answer.

First look at commercially made (bought) pasta, a good convenience food both in its dried and fresh forms. Several kinds have potential *if they are available*. The first is soup pastas because they are small shapes. Some are really tiny and do not need to be chewed. They are more expensive than the average-sized pastas.

Anelli, 'rings'.
Orzo, 'barley'—resembles rice.
Pastina, 'tiny dough'—a whole range of small pastas for soup. Some may not be small enough.
Stellini, 'little stars'.
Stellete—tiny flower shapes.

When buying, bear in mind that they will swell a little during cooking.

The second kind of pasta with potential for soft options is a type of dried noodles called *capelli d'angelo*, 'angel hair'. They are extremely fine and usually come in a kind of 'nest' of noodles, as does *vermicelli*. For more about these, see *Cooking dried noodles*, p. 64.

When cooking the soup pastas or the fine noodles they need to be strained in a fine mesh sieve, not a colander, or they will slip through the holes.

Cooked pasta, whether fresh or dried, does not respond well to a food processor or mini-chopper, due to its tendency to be slippery. Even chopping by hand is difficult as the pieces tend to stick together in an ever-enlarging clump. However, cutting it up *before* it is cooked is relatively easy, but only if you use fresh pasta, not dried. The latter will just shatter under a knife but can be dealt with in another way as you will see.

It is possible to buy ready-made fresh noodles or lasagne. These can be cut into tiny squares and cooked but are not a patch on homemade versions and may turn out to be too tough.

Brown pasta

Pasta made with brown flour has a distinctive nutty taste compared with traditional white pasta which is fairly bland. Brown pasta dough is weaker and not so easy to make as white. Make sure you use a finely ground wholewheat flour and when rolling out make it into smaller pieces than for the white. You will need a really sharp knife for cutting it up.

There are several advantages to making your own pasta. It is inexpensive, easily made, cooks quickly and merely requires a rolling-pin and knife to make it. If too much is made it can be cooked and then frozen for future use. By using sunflower oil instead of olive oil a softer pasta can be made. By avoiding strong flour and using just ordinary plain flour the result is a less chewy pasta.

Cooking tiny dried pasta shapes

Bought dried pasta shapes such as tiny *stellete* take longer to cook than fresh ones. However, 7 or 8 minutes should be ample. About 3–4oz (80–100g) make a good-size portion. Bring about 3 pints (1½ litres) water to the boil in a large pan. Add 2 pinches salt and sprinkle in the pasta shapes. Stir and cook for a minute, then stir again. Finish cooking and drain in a fine mesh sieve. Return to the hot, empty pan and put in a knob of butter or margarine. Stir until melted and serve.

If you want to use dried pasta (for convenience) and are unable to buy the tiny pasta shapes, consider flat sheets of lasagne which can be cut into tiny squares after partly cooking, albeit with difficulty. Avoid the ridged types as they will be too difficult to handle. After five minutes' cooking in a pan of boiling water, take out the lasagne sheets with a slotted spoon, drain in a colander and lay out on a cutting board. Cut into thin strips, then cut across to make tiny squares. Put back into the pan and finish cooking until soft. Drain in a fine mesh sieve and put back into the empty pan with a small knob of butter. Stir and serve with an appropriate sauce (see chapter 6).

Cooking dried noodles

First make your tiny noodles. Take a 'nest' of dried vermicelli or even finer noodles (spaghetti is too tough). Put between two double sheets of kitchen paper and press hard with a rolling-pin. Expect a loud cracking and crunching noise as the noodles break. Keep re-rolling until all the noodles have broken into short lengths. Put into a basin and shake—all the longest pieces will come to the top. These can be removed and rolled again to make them smaller. Put to one side while you make more tiny noodles. When you have as much as you need, pour into a pan of boiling water and cook for three minutes. Drain in a fine mesh sieve. Put back into the empty pan with a small knob of butter, stir and serve with an appropriate sauce.

HINTS: The first time you tackle any of these solutions to soft options pasta it will seem to take ages. The next time you'll be quicker at it and gradually, as your skill improves, you'll settle to it and will be able to do it quite quickly and easily. It is worth working at it as a wide range of soft sauces can be made to go with it. If the pasta is small enough it won't need chewing.

- For taste make homemade pasta and cut into tiny squares.
- For convenience make vermicelli or finer noodles into short lengths.
- Take a whole packet of vermicelli and make into tiny noodles. Store in a jar for later use. You will need to replace the kitchen paper frequently during rolling as it will wear out quickly.
- Buy the tiniest pasta shapes.
- If desperate buy fresh lasagne or tagliatelle and cut it up into little squares before cooking.
- If *really* desperate, parcook dried lasagne and cut up into tiny squares, then finish cooking.

Pasta for tiny squares

This recipe makes 2 portions. Avoid flour labelled 'strong' or 'for pasta'.

3oz (80g) plain white flour or	½ beaten egg
fine grade wholemeal	1½ tablespoons sunflower oil
3 pinches salt	cold water

Method: Mix the flour and salt in a bowl. Make a well in the centre. Mix the egg and oil in a cup using a fork. Pour into the well. Use the fork to stir the liquid into the flour. Add a little water to make a soft dough. Knead on a floured worktop for about 5 minutes until the dough has become shiny and smooth. Wrap it in greaseproof paper and leave it to rest for 10 minutes.

Flour the worktop and roll out the dough in two lots. Keep rolling and dusting with flour until the pasta is as thin as paper. Pick it up on the rolling-pin and dust the worktop with flour. Put the pasta on top and dust lightly. Cover with food film and leave for another 10 minutes. Brush off excess flour and with a sharp knife cut into long, thin noodles. Gather into a neat bundle and cut into tiny squares by slicing across the strips. The knife should be sharp enough to cut through the dough without being pressed too hard, otherwise the squares will all stick together. Hold the bundle of noodles lightly so as not to press them together. Sprinkle the squares onto a floured plate as you make them.

Have ready a large pan of boiling water. Put in the pasta squares and boil rapidly for 2–3 minutes when they will be cooked. Drain in a wire sieve and put back in the hot saucepan with a knob of butter or margarine. Stir gently. Serve half with a suitable sauce (see chapter 6 for sauces to go with the pasta squares).

NOTE: As the tiny squares will increase slightly in size during cooking, you may find them too large. Put on a board and chop smaller with a large knife or mezzaluna.

Pasta Verdi (green pasta) for tiny squares
Makes enough for 3 portions (less would not be economical).

| 8oz (225g) white flour | 1½oz cooked spinach (fresh) |
| 1½ eggs, beaten | 2 pinches salt |

Method: Purée the spinach in a liquidiser with a little of the cooking liquid. Put into a fine mesh sieve and press with the back of a spoon to squeeze out water and make the spinach as dry as possible. Mix the flour and salt in a bowl. Make a well in the centre and pour in the beaten egg. Use a fork to stir the liquid into the flour. Mix in the puréed spinach and add a little water, if necessary, to make a soft, green dough. Knead on a floured worktop for 4 to 5 minutes until the dough is smooth and shiny. Roll out as thin as paper on a floured worktop. Use a sharp knife to cut into thin strips then cut across the strips to make tiny pasta squares. Sprinkle a little flour on a dinner plate and scatter the squares on the plate as you make them. When they are all made, put into a large pan of boiling water with 2 pinches of salt. Cook steadily for about 3 to 4 minutes. Strain and serve hot with a suitable sauce (see chapter 6).

COUSCOUS

This is a useful, rather bland, high carbohydrate food. It is made from wheat and sold as minute dry grains which need to be reconstituted and then cooked. Serve instead of rice, pasta or potatoes as it doesn't need chewing. Health food shops will have it in white or brown, supermarkets usually have it in white. A store-cupboard standby.

Steamed Couscous (1 serving)

2oz (50g) couscous	pinch salt
4fl oz (125ml) boiling water	1 teaspoon sunflower oil

Method: Put the couscous into a small saucepan. Pour the boiling water over it and stir in the salt and oil. Put on the lid and leave to stand for about 5 minutes so that the couscous can swell. Put into a fine mesh wire sieve. Have ready a pan one third full of boiling water. Put the sieve over the pan and steam for about 6 or 7 minutes. Fork up the couscous to keep the grains separate and serve hot with meat dishes or cold with salads.

NOTE: It is possible to reconstitute and heat the couscous by leaving it to stand for 15 minutes instead of 5. Omit the steaming.

PASTRY

Avoid milk or egg wash as a finish, and do not sprinkle with granulated or demerara sugar.

Soft Potato Pastry
This is a useful pastry for quiches, as an alternative to ordinary pastry which may have to be made into crumbs.

5oz (130g) plain wholewheat flour	4oz (100g) cold mashed potato
1 level teaspoon baking powder	3oz (80g) polyunsaturated margarine

Preheat oven: Gas 4/180°C/350°F. *Position*: top shelf. *Baking time*: 30 minutes or less.

Method: Mix the flour and baking powder in a bowl. Add the mashed potato. Mix again and put in the margarine. Blend with a fork and knead on a floured worktop. Roll out, using more flour, and use to line a flan dish or as a savoury pie topping.

Soft Pastry

As white flour produces a crisper pastry than brown it seems sensible to use the latter. Brown pastry has a distinct 'nutty' flavour. It is more difficult to handle than white but produces softer pastry.

4oz (100g) plain wholewheat flour	2oz (50g) soft margarine water

Preheat oven: Gas 6/200°C/400°F. *Position*: top shelf. *Baking time*: 15–20 minutes (do not allow it to become too crisp).

Method: In a bowl rub in the margarine and flour. When the mixture resembles breadcrumbs, add enough water to mix to a wet paste. Use more flour to bring the paste back to a soft texture that can be rolled out. Use more flour on the worktop and the rolling-pin. Roll out not too thinly. Use for either sweet or savoury dishes.

Biscuit Pastry

Use for the base of lemon meringue pie and cheesecake.

2oz (50g) soft margarine	2oz (50g) caster sugar
5oz (130g) digestive biscuits	

Method: Make the biscuits into fine crumbs in a coffee grinder. Melt the margarine in a saucepan. Stir in the biscuit crumbs and sugar. Press into flan tin, over the base and up the sides. Leave to set in the fridge.

NOTE: People experiencing sore mouth, tongue or throat may find this pastry too rough.

Pancakes (2 servings)

2oz (50g) plain flour (white)	1 slightly heaped tablespoon low-fat dried milk granules
small pinch of salt	
1 small egg, beaten	sunflower oil
¼pt (150ml) water	

Method: Put the flour, salt, egg, water and dried milk into a liquidiser. Blend to a smooth, creamy batter. Heat a 6in (15cm) omelette pan

67

and put in a few drops of oil. Spread all over the pan with a screw of kitchen paper. Pour in about a tablespoon of batter and tilt the pan so that the batter covers the base evenly. Cook for a minute, until the base is speckled with brown, then turn over and cook on the other side for about 30 seconds. Turn on to a warm plate and cover with a tea towel. The pancake will go from crisp to limp. Make the rest of the batter into pancakes and stack one on top of the other. Keep warm.

Pancakes can be shredded with a large knife, on a board, then cut across to make tiny squares.

Dumplings (2–3 servings)
These make a good substitute for potatoes and can be flavoured with herbs. Use on top of stews and soups. They are light and soft.

2oz (50g) plain flour (white or brown)	½ egg, beaten
2 pinches salt	finely chopped herb (optional, see list below)
1 level teaspoon baking powder	milk to mix
2oz (50g) soft margarine	

Method: Put the flour, salt and baking powder into a basin. Rub in the margarine. Mix together the optional herb and egg. Stir into the flour mixture. Gradually add a little milk to make a stiff dough. Flour your hands and break off small pieces to roll into balls the size of marbles. With a floured knife cut each one into four and roll into even smaller balls. Drop them over your bubbling stew or soup and put on the lid for about 10 minutes while cooking continues.

Herbs: Choose from 1 tablespoon finely chopped parsley, 2 teaspoons finely chopped thyme or mixed herbs.

NOTE: The dumplings will double in size during cooking but should still be really small. Try not to compress them too much when you roll them. If making tiny dumplings is too fiddly, roll dough into balls the size of marbles. Cook for 20 minutes. Remove with a slotted spoon and cut each one in half then into neat quarters.

Soft Stuffing (1 serving)

Method: Make 1 slice of bread into crumbs in a coffee grinder. Grease a small, shallow ovenproof dish with a lid. Finely chop ¼ of a medium onion and fresh herb(s) to make 1 slightly heaped teaspoon (see suggestions below). Mix crumbs, onion and herbs in the dish with 1 tablespoon sunflower oil and enough water to make a wet consistency. Season to taste with salt and fine pepper. Bake with the lid on along with a joint of pork or chicken until most of the liquid has dried out but the stuffing is still soft. If preferred, cook in a saucepan on the hob, stirring for a few minutes until the correct texture is achieved. Keep warm, covered, until required. The onion can be fried in the oil first to make it more easily digested.

Suggestions

1 1 teaspoon fresh sage or ½ teaspoon dried.
2 1 teaspoon fresh thyme or ½ teaspoon dried and finely grated rind of ¼ lemon.
3 1 teaspoon fresh mixed herbs or ½ teaspoon dried.

CHAPTER 5

Breakfasts and Juices

The idea of breakfast, as the name suggests, is to end the overnight fast and get a good start to the day. Many people avoid breakfast altogether and eat their first food of the day at mid-morning or later. Common sense will tell you it is not sensible to go without food for twelve hours or more. For people with physical or tiring jobs breakfasts need to be hearty, but usually a light meal is eaten as it is early in the day and food must be prepared and eaten quickly. Most of it is chewy, and if you look at the following list of possibles you will see the problem-free foods are few compared to the chewy ones (problem foods are in italics).

Breakfast cereals, porridge, *muesli*, milk, sugar.
Rolls, bread, toast, crispbread, muffins (USA), croissants.
Pancakes.
Cheese, eggs, sausages, bacon, fried bread, ham, fish, potato, mush-rooms, tomatoes.
Jam, honey, *marmalade*, butter, margarine.
Fruit or fruit juice.
Yoghurt.

All kinds of solutions follow, but first, a look at yoghurt.

FLAVOURED YOGHURT

There was a time when yoghurt was unobtainable. If you wanted it you had to make it yourself at home. Now it is everywhere in a multitude of flavours. Potentially it is a healthy food, but the food technologists have seen to it that, in some forms, it has become a serious junk food high in fat and sugar, bristling with additives, colouring and chemicals. If you wish to avoid these hazards buy low-fat, unflavoured 'bio' yoghurt and flavour it yourself at home. There is no need for artificial flavours, colours and chemicals to give it long shelf-life. Just use correctly prepared fruit and perhaps a little sweetening.

Method: For each serving put 2 to 2½ heaped tablespoons unflavoured, low-fat yoghurt into a small bowl. Stir in the fruit or flavouring from the list that follows. Taste and sweeten if necessary with a little sugar or runny honey. Avoid too much sweetening as the fruit or flavouring should take precedence and ripe, sweet fruit should not really require any sweetening.

Apricot—2–3 stewed apricots, stones removed and processed in a mini-chopper. Stir into yoghurt.
Banana—mash ½ a ripe banana on a plate with a few drops of lemon juice. Mix yoghurt into banana.
Blackberry—as for blackcurrant (see below).
Blackberry and apple—as for blackcurrant but add a tablespoon of stewed apple.
Blackcurrant—stew 1 heaped tablespoon of blackcurrants until soft, putting in as little water as possible. Put through a fine mesh sieve and stir into the yoghurt.
Blueberries—use 1 heaped tablespoon processed in a mini-chopper with 1 tablespoon of the yoghurt. Spoon into a dish and add more yoghurt.
Chocolate—stir together 1 slightly heaped teaspoon drinking chocolate and 1 drop of vanilla flavouring. Stir into yoghurt.
Coffee—mix 1 level teaspoon instant coffee into 2 teaspoons boiling water. Allow to cool before mixing into yoghurt.
Guava—use 2 halves from a can. Pick out the pips which are very hard. Chop the flesh finely or put into a mini-processor with a tablespoon of the yoghurt. Process and add more yoghurt.
Mango—1 heaped tablespoon puréed ripe mango, either fresh or drained canned. Stir into yoghurt.
Nectarine—as for peach (see below).
Passion fruit—cut a fruit in half and scoop out the centre with a

71

teaspoon. Put through a fine mesh sieve. The small amount of purée is very strong-flavoured. Stir into yoghurt.

Pawpaw—halve a ripe fruit and scoop out and discard the tiny black seeds. Spoon out the flesh onto a plate. Mash with a fork. Add to the yoghurt, folding rather than mixing it in. The flavour is delicate and requires half a fruit.

Peach—peel and remove stone. Use half, finely chopped. The fruit must be ripe and soft. Stir into yoghurt.

Peach and raspberry—use ¼ of a peeled ripe peach, finely chopped, and 6–8 raspberries, mashed with a fork and put through a fine sieve to remove pips.

Peach and redcurrant—use ¼ of a peeled, ripe peach, finely chopped, and 1 tablespoon redcurrants stewed, mashed and put through a sieve. If you don't have any fresh redcurrants, try a tablespoon of redcurrant jelly, chopped and stirred into yoghurt.

Pear—either use half a ripe pear peeled and cored, or 2 canned pear quarters, drained. Process in a mini-chopper or chop very finely with a knife. Stir into yoghurt.

Pear and cinnamon—make as for pear but add 2 or 3 pinches cinnamon.

Pineapple—use 5 or 6 chunks from a can (drained) or ½ fresh pineapple ring. Chop, then put in a mini-chopper and process. Stir into yoghurt.

Plum—peel 1 stewed or 1 fresh ripe, eating plum. Cut out the stone. Chop the flesh finely or process in a mini-chopper. Stir into yoghurt.

Prune—Use either 3 stoned prunes you have cooked yourself or 3 canned fruit, stones removed. Process in a mini-chopper. Fold into the yoghurt.

Prune and lemon—make as for prune, adding ¼ teaspoon finely grated lemon rind. Stir into yoghurt.

Raspberry—mash about 8–10 fresh raspberries. Put through a fine mesh sieve and stir into yoghurt.

Strawberry—3 large strawberries, peeled with a sharp knife to remove pips. Mash what is left on a plate using a fork. Stir into yoghurt. (See chapter 3 for more about the peeling of strawberries.)

Vanilla—add a few drops of vanilla flavouring. Stir into yoghurt.

BREAKFAST CEREALS

Any cereal with extra bran, nuts or fruit will be chewy and so will very dry kinds. While soaking in milk will reduce cereal to a mush it won't necessarily soften it enough to dispense with chewing and it certainly won't make any impression on the nuts or dried fruit. Having reduced cereal to a sloppy, non-chew consistency, does it have appeal? Some people think so.

Try reducing non-crunchy, plain cereal to crumbs in a coffee grinder (Weetabix will crumble by hand). Soak in milk to soften. Serve with a little sugar. Allow at least 15 minutes for the soaking when the liquid will be taken up by the cereal crumbs. Add a little more milk if it turns out too thick.

Porridge

This is the breakfast cereal institutions like to serve as it is cheap and can be kept warm for ages. However, very few know how to make it well and it tends to turn out too thin or too thick.

Although it seems like a soft food when made, the rolled oats are quite large, and combined with a sticky texture it can be an uncomfortable food to eat. Here is a better solution with the rolled oats reduced to crumbs before cooking.

Quick Oat Porridge (1 serving)

2 slightly heaped tablespoons   ⅔ teacup hot water
    rolled oats   skimmed milk and brown sugar
pinch of salt   to serve

Method: Put the oats into a coffee grinder. Grind to a powder and turn into a small saucepan (preferably non-stick). Add the salt and quickly pour in the water. Mix while you heat for a minute. Take off the heat and beat to a smooth consistency. Spoon into a serving bowl. Pour over a little milk and sprinkle with brown sugar. For a treat use less milk to serve and replace with a tablespoon of single cream.

Variation: Add one tablespoon of wheat bran.

Rice Porridge (1–2 servings)

People who dislike oat porridge might prefer this fairly bland breakfast dish.

2 generous tablespoons ground   2 tablespoons sunflower oil
    rice   sugar or honey to taste
½pt (300ml) skimmed milk

Method: Put the rice and milk into a small saucepan and stir until smooth. Mix in the oil and bring to the boil while stirring. Turn down the heat and continue to stir for 3 or 4 minutes. Take off the heat and stir in sweetening to taste. Serve hot with skimmed milk poured over.

Variations: Stir in 1 tablespoon finely ground almonds before serving. 1 tablespoon sultanas or seedless raisins can be added. Soak in half a cup of boiling water for a few minutes, then drain and chop as finely as you can.

Bread and Milk

There are all kinds of names for this old-fashioned form of breakfast cereal—everything from 'sops' to 'goody'. It is incredibly cheap and easy to make and is what many people ate before breakfast cereals were available.

Cut a slice of soft bread. Remove the crusts and cut what is left into small cubes. Put into a dish and pour over hot, skimmed milk. The bread will take up the milk and soften completely. Sprinkle with a little sugar or drizzle with runny honey to taste. If there is not much taste to the bread a pinch or two of cinnamon will give it a lift, as will a tablespoon of single cream.

TYPICAL BREAKFAST FOODS

Jam and marmalade—no bits of peel means jelly marmalade (see chapter 14 for information and recipes). Cut slices of soft bread. Cut off crusts, spread with butter or soft margarine and jelly jam or marmalade. Cut into small squares.

Bread, rolls—see chapter 4 for special soft breads and how to serve them for soft options.

Toast—this has a special taste. Make toast, reduce to crumbs in a coffee grinder. Use mixed with melted butter or soft margarine with cooked breakfasts.

Crispbreads—reduce to crumbs in a coffee grinder. The resulting dry crumbs must be mixed with water or milk as appropriate. This is a compromise but it will *taste* of crispbread for those with a craving for it.

Croissants—chop on a board, as finely as you can. Serve in a dish with a teaspoon. Nothing like the complete croissant but with all the taste.

Pancakes—see chapter 4 for recipe and instructions.

Muffins—these are popular in the USA for a late breakfast or brunch. See p. 160 for Cup Cakes. Bake fresh but avoid icing. The ones with fruit in are most typical, not the flavoured buns.

Cheese—cottage cheese can be put through a fine mesh sieve.

Bacon—grill bacon until crisp. Chop into small pieces and pulverise with a pestle and mortar. Use to sprinkle over scrambled, poached or fried egg, and special mushrooms (see below).

Fried bread—make bread into soft crumbs. Fry in a little sunflower oil. Don't let it get too crisp.

Ham—see chapter 9 for soft ham slices.

Fish—boil-in-the-bag *kippers* will be the softest. Choose fillets, cook as instructions. Turn out on to a warmed plate and mash. Pick out any bones that are obvious. Drizzle with a little melted butter and serve with small squares of soft, buttered brown bread, crusts cut off.

Poach *smoked haddock* in milk. Drain and mash. Shape into a circle on a warmed plate. Top with a soft poached egg. Chop up with a knife as small as you can. Serve with soft buttered brown bread. See also savoury fish cakes, p. 138. Serve with sieved canned tomatoes.

Potato—use cold boiled potato. Mash and fry in a little sunflower oil.

Mushrooms—these are inclined to be rubbery and difficult to chew. Chop really finely on a board, using a large knife. Fry in a little sunflower oil. Drain in a fine sieve.

Tomato—see p. 40 for how to skin and de-seed. Chop remaining flesh and heat through in a pan. Sprinkle with a pinch of sugar, salt and fine pepper. Serve with fish cakes and other cooked breakfasts.

EGGS

Please read the notes in chapter 2 about eating eggs.

Baked Egg (1 serving)

This is probably the most delicious way to eat an egg, providing it is a free range one with a good flavour. Liberally grease a ramekin (cocotte) with soft margarine. Have ready a roasting tin half-filled with boiling water. Break an egg into the prepared dish. Place it in the hot water and put the roasting tin on the top shelf of a pre-heated oven Gas 4/180°C/350°F. Bake for about 8 minutes or less, until the white has set but the yolk is still runny. Cut up with a knife while still in the dish. Serve with a teaspoon and tiny squares of soft bread and butter or soft margarine.

Scrambled Eggs (1 serving)
In principle this is a soft dish. In practice it isn't, as people warm it up in the microwave and generally overcook it, making it really tough and impossible to chew. Allow only a minute between making and serving and never overcook it.

small knob soft margarine   1 fresh, free range egg
1 tablespoon skimmed milk

Method: Melt the margarine gently in a small non-stick pan. Add the milk and break in the egg. Keep over a low heat and, as it cooks, break the egg up with a wooden spoon. Gradually the egg will set. When it is still a little runny and still looks shiny take off the heat (it will continue to cook with the warmth of the pan). A tablespoon of single cream stirred in before serving will make it very special but is not essential. Spoon on to a warm serving plate and serve with soft bread and butter or soft margarine or fried mashed potato.

NOTE: The foolproof way to make scrambled egg is in a double boiler, i.e. a small pan over a larger pan containing simmering water.

Fried Egg
Overcooking this simple food will make it tough and rubbery with a crisp edge nobody can chew. Heat a tablespoon of sunflower oil in a frying-pan. Break in an egg and fry over a gentle heat. When the white has set underneath, carefully turn over with a fish slice and cook on the other side. Lift out on to a board. Carefully cut out round the yolk, leaving on a thin ring of the white. Chop the white finely and arrange on a plate in a circle. Now mash the yolk with a fork or cut it up with a knife. Spoon it into the circle of white. This is preferable to chopping both up together in an unrecognisable mush.

For bacon and egg, sprinkle the prepared bacon over the chopped egg white. See p. 75 for preparation of bacon.

Poached Egg
Pour hot water into a small non-stick saucepan or frying-pan to a depth of 1 inch (2.5cm). Heat to boiling point and then break in an egg. Simmer until the white has set and the yolk looks cloudy. Present in the same way as a fried egg (above).

Omelette

Although compared with meat an omelette is soft, alas it is not soft enough for soft options. It is in fact quite a chewy food, especially if it has been allowed to cool down. For the desperate non-chewer addicted to omelettes, make and serve immediately. On no account cook the omelette too much or it will be leathery. It can be cut up into small squares if this is an easier way to eat it. Put on a large chopping board and cut into strips with a large chopping knife. Then cut across to make squares. It must be done quickly as the omelette will rapidly cool down. Transfer to a warm serving plate, using a spatula, and serve immediately. For a filled omelette put a layer of half the little squares on the plate, cover with a soft filling and top with the remaining squares.

Plain Omelette (1 serving)

1 egg
2 tablespoons cold water

small knob of soft margarine or
butter

Method: Beat the egg and water in a cup, using a fork. Heat a small omelette pan and put in the margarine or butter to melt. When it is sizzling, pour in the egg. Tip the pan one way then the other to let the mixture settle evenly as the bottom cooks. Break the omelette in places to let the still runny egg set in the gaps. Use a fish slice to turn one half over the other and slide out on to a warmed serving plate. Serve immediately.

Filled Omelette

Make as for plain omelette, but before folding spread a soft filling over one half. Any of the following fillings are soft and suitable.

Cheese—sprinkle over 1 slightly heaped tablespoon finely grated tasty cheddar cheese, or spoon over 2 tablespoons of cheese sauce.
Tomato—see p. 40 for how to skin and de-seed tomatoes. Chop the flesh of 2 tomatoes, season with a pinch or two of caster sugar, salt and fine pepper.
Bacon and mushroom—prepare both as suggested on p. 75.
Mushroom—finely chop a medium-sized mushroom. Fry in a little melted soft margarine. Stir in a tablespoon of single cream. Season to taste.
Ham—finely chop a thin slice of lean ham using a large chopping knife (reduce it to crumbs the size of sawdust). Mix with 2 teaspoons of single cream.

Mushrooms, Bacon and Fried Bread

Cook mushrooms and bacon separately (see p. 75). Make soft bread into crumbs and fry lightly in a little sunflower oil. Put on to a warmed serving plate. Spoon over the mushrooms and sprinkle on the bacon. Tremendous taste!

Skinless Pork Sausages (makes 8 small sausages for 2 servings)

about 3oz (80g) lean pork fillet	1 teaspoon sunflower oil
1oz (25g) soft breadcrumbs	pinch allspice
½ medium cooking apple	pinch mixed herbs
2 teaspoons soy sauce	flour for coating
finely ground pepper to taste	sunflower oil for frying

Method: Trim off all fat and gristle from the pork. Chop the meat into small pieces and put them through a mincer or process in a mini-chopper. Peel and core the cooking apple. Grate finely. Put all the ingredients except the flour and frying oil into a basin. Mix well. Form into small sausage shapes and roll in flour. Fry in a little, hot sunflower oil, turning once, for a total of 5 minutes. Avoid making them crisp but make sure they are cooked right through. Serve with sieved canned tomatoes.

NOTE: Bought sausages usually have plastic skins which require chewing. For sausage fans multiply up the recipe and make extra for freezing.

JUICES

Fresh juices have a life-force which makes them a potent and enjoyable source of vitamins and minerals. Instead of taking hours to be assimilated by the body, as does solid food, juices take only minutes. When people are very weak, juices would seem to be more suitable than food as a source of nourishment.

The only way to use fresh, unadulterated juices is to make them yourself. The commercial variety are usually just concoctions composed mainly of water which is flavoured, preserved and coloured, resulting in juices of uncertain age. As few people know what fresh juice is like, introducing them may be a pleasant surprise.

Fresh fruit and vegetable juices should be sipped slowly, preferably from a teaspoon or through a straw. They are very strong sources of nutrients and must not be drunk or gulped down quickly. Ideal for serving between meals, at elevenses, during the day, or as a nightcap, they need to be sipped within minutes of making, except for grape juice. Some, such as apple or pear and carrot, will start to discolour immediately. A squeeze of fresh lemon juice stirred in will delay this.

Fresh juices

All the fruits and vegetables listed below can be used for juices:

Fruits	*Vegetables*
apple	beetroot
apricot	carrot
banana	celery
grape	cucumber
grapefruit	lettuce
lemon	parsley
mango	spinach
nectarine	watercress
orange	
passion fruit	
pawpaw	
peach	
pear	
pineapple	
plum	
prune	
raisin	
raspberry	
strawberry	
tomato	

Apricot, prune and raisin are dried but the remainder are fresh and raw. Grapefruit, orange and lemon are easily squeezed out on a citrus press but the rest need to be used in a juicer. As well as single juices, blends can be made. Grape is a loner and is best served on its own. It has the advantage of being the only juice that does not deteriorate drastically if stored in the fridge for two or three days.

Not all juices are compatible for taste. The following should *not* be combined: prune, citrus or apricot with green leaves; beetroot with berries; pear with tomato. These mixtures are completely undrinkable!

Of all the juices, three make a really good base for mixing with another juice. They are apple, orange and carrot. A little runny honey or sugar to taste can be added if sweetening is required. In spite of putting what seems to be a large amount of fruit or vegetables through the juicer, only a small amount of juice results. However, as the flavour will be intense it can be diluted with water. Some fruits, such as blackcurrants, are just too expensive to juice, and not all vegetables are suitable, for example potatoes, peas and beans. Citrus fruits can be peeled and put through a juicer as well as pressed and juiced. Their great advantage if taken fresh is their vitamin C content. Pineapple and banana are best suited to a blender but can also be put through a juicer (the banana will need to be soaked overnight in water).

Fruit and vegetables for juicing should always be fresh. Don't bother with stale, wilty-looking items as they won't give good results. Always wash ingredients well before using. A stiff brush for removing dirt is useful. Cut out and discard any bruised or damaged parts before juicing. Berries can be rinsed in a colander under the cold tap.

PREPARATION FOR JUICING

Fruit

Apple—cut into quarters including skin, core and pips and put through a juicer.

Apricot—soak dried halves overnight in plenty of cold water, put through a juicer with the soaking water and a squeeze of lemon juice (high in iron).

Banana—peel and soak in cold water overnight, put through juicer with the soaking water (high in potassium).

Grape—choose seedless varieties, remove stalks before using.

Grapefruit—cut in half and use a citrus juicer, or peel and pull into segments to put through juicer (high in vitamin C).

Lemon—as for grapefruit (high in vitamin C).

Mango—peel, halve and cut flesh away from central stone, put flesh through juicer. May need to be diluted well or mixed with apple, flavour is intense.

Nectarine—halve and remove stone, put through juicer.

Orange—as for grapefruit (high in vitamin C).

Passion fruit—being such a small fruit, halve and scoop out pulp with a teaspoon. Put through a small, fine wire sieve if you don't want the pips. Only a small amount is produced but flavour is intense.

Pawpaw—halve and scoop out seeds with a spoon and discard; peel and chop, liquidise with water and blend.

Peach—halve and remove stone, slice and put through juicer.

80

Pear—as for apple.

Pineapple—cut off top and bottom, quarter lengthways and cut away and discard the core. Cut remaining flesh away from the skin and chop into pieces. Put into liquidiser with water and blend. Dilute to taste (good aid to digestion).

Plum—halve and remove stones using only ripe, soft fruit, put through juicer (good laxative).

Prune—soak overnight in plenty of cold water, remove stones and put through juicer with soaking water (good laxative).

Raisin—soak overnight using seedless dried fruit, put through juicer with the soaking water (high in iron).

Raspberry—hull and put through juicer; will mix well with apple.

Strawberry—as for raspberry.

Tomato—cut into quarters and put through juicer.

Vegetables

Beetroot—avoid old beets; top, tail and peel, keeping leaves if not wilting, cut into small chunks and put through juicer. Blend immediately with pineapple juice (equal parts) to preserve the incredible ruby wine colour.

Carrot—an exceptionally nutritious vegetable high in vitamin A (as beta carotene) and a good mixer. Unless using organic carrots, peel thinly, top and tail. Cut into chunks and put through juicer.

Celery—use leaves as well as stalks; the stalks must be cut into short lengths before putting through juicer.

Cucumber—do not peel, chop into chunks and put through juicer (a natural diuretic, and a refreshing hot-weather drink).

Lettuce—use non-bitter varieties, include outside leaves, put through juicer and combine 1 part lettuce juice with 2 parts carrot juice to make it palatable (good source of iron).

Parsley—break into sprigs and put through juicer followed by carrot or celery. The parsley juice will be bitter, and a mixture of 7 parts celery or carrot to 1 part parsley is preferable.

Spinach—put young leaves through the juicer. The juice will be very strong-tasting and 1 part should be diluted with 2 parts carrot juice (good for the digestive tract).

Watercress—put extra well washed leaves and stalks through the juicer. A very strong taste: mix with 7 parts celery or carrot juice.

Amounts

Do not expect more than half a cup of juice from three or four large carrots. A whole pineapple put through the juicer does well to make half a cup. However, this kind of extracted juice should not be compared with the pulped and diluted commercial kind—there is no resemblance. Bear in mind that only small amounts should be taken, in other words, please don't think it is drunk by the half pint.

Generally speaking, put the equivalent of two to four portions through the juicer per serving. For example, use three or four apples to make one serving. Fruit and vegetables which contain a high proportion of water, such as tomatoes, will produce a more generous amount of juice than, say, peaches. You may like to keep a notebook of how much you put through the juicer each time to make a serving, rather than just keep guessing.

Juices from canned fruit

Obviously, juices made from canned fruit will not be as high in nutrients as the fresh versions. Most canned fruit is cooked, but it is easily digested and saves time in preparation. It is unusual for it to have additives except for sugar, and compared with the pretend fresh fruit juices sold in waxed cartons it is much better value for money and relatively little processed. For canned fruit there is no season and it is easily stored on a shelf.

Not all canned fruit is really suitable for making into a juice. Strawberries, cherries, fruits of the forest (a mixture of raspberries, strawberries, blackberries, blueberries, cherries and redcurrants), mandarin oranges, rhubarb, loganberries, fruit salads and fruit cocktail come into this category. Raspberries and blackcurrants are not a great success either; the frozen versions can be stewed to produce a much better juice.

Canned fruits come in syrup (sugar and water), plain water or fruit juices. However they are packed, strain off the liquid and just use the fruit unless indicated.

Single fruit juices (from canned fruit)

Pears, peaches, apricots, pineapple and guavas
About half the fruit from a medium-sized can or all the fruit from a small one will make a generous-sized drink for one. Strain the fruit and put into a liquidiser goblet. Top up with a cup of cold water and blend. Put through a fine mesh sieve, sweeten to taste, dilute with more water if necessary and serve in a tumbler.

Lychees, mangoes, blackberries, plums and prunes
The exotic fruits like lychees and mangoes, and the less exotic blackberries, plums and prunes, all have a strong taste and either need to be greatly diluted or mixed with apple juice. Remove any

stones and proceed as for single fruit juices, but use ¼ of a medium can or ½ a small can including the liquid. Dilute with water and/or apple juice to taste after blending.

Grapefruit
Many people find grapefruit juice causes indigestion, especially if taken on an empty stomach. However, those who don't have a problem with it should enjoy canned fruit and its liquid blended to make juice. Use a brand with a good name for the best quality, rather than a supermarket own brand. It might not need diluting or sweetening. Taste and see.

Juices from stewed fruit
Prepare and stew in a little water any of these fresh fruits: raspberries, blackberries, loganberries, redcurrants, blackcurrants, apricots, plums, damsons, cherries, greengages, gooseberries. Cook until soft, remove stones (if any). Blend in a liquidiser and put through a fine sieve. Sweeten and dilute to taste. Store in a screwtop jar in the fridge for not more than two days before consuming. Serve the currant and berry juices in small amounts, diluted with water, apple or pineapple juice, as the flavours are strong.

Juice from frozen fruit
Stew frozen raspberries, blackberries, blackcurrants or fruits of the forest in water, then proceed as above.

SHAKES

People who have never taken breakfast and cannot face food first thing sometimes respond to a 'shake'. With a base of milk or yoghurt, all kinds of fruit combinations can be blended in a liquidiser. Honey or a little sugar can be used to sweeten and an interesting variety is possible. Here are three typical examples.

Breakfast Shake
Into the blender goblet put 1 small carton (or 1 portion) of natural (unflavoured) yoghurt, 1 small banana, 4 or 5 strawberries* or raspberries and a small ripe pear or apple (peeled, cored and sliced). Blend until smooth. Put through a fine mesh sieve. Sip slowly.

* May not be suitable for everyone due to the tiny pips (see p. 40).

Banana Milk Shake
Blend the following: 1 small banana, 2 cups water, 3 level table-spoons low-fat dried milk granules, 1 generous teaspoon honey or soft brown sugar. Drink slowly, sipping through a straw—this is food!

Other ripe fresh fruits to use are:

peaches	plums
nectarines	pineapple
apricots	mango
pawpaw	seedless grapes

If you use fruit with skins, put the resulting shake through a fine mesh sieve. The advantage of using dried milk as opposed to fresh is that juices can be used as a liquid base, for example pineapple or apple, instead of whole milk.

Pineapple Milk Shake
Blend the following until smooth: 2 cups canned pineapple juice, 3 tablespoons low-fat dried milk powder, soft brown sugar or liquid honey to taste (optional). Sip slowly.

Other juices to use are: pear, apple, grape, peach, apricot—the list is endless.

CHAPTER 6

Sauces, Gravies and Dressings

These are of the utmost important for soft options food as they help with the essential moistness of dishes, making swallowing easier. They can also bring out flavours from other food and are used to complement meat, fish, vegetables and salads. A great anti-boredom factor, especially for the more subtle flavours of fish, TVP and potatoes which can often be desperate for variety.

SAUCES

Basic White Sauce (2 servings)

2 heaped tablespoons low-fat
    dried milk granules

½pt (300ml) cold water
1 level tablespoon cornflour

Method: Mix the dried milk into the water. Put the cornflour into a jug and add 3 tablespoons of the milk. Stir until smooth then gradually add the remaining milk. Pour into a small heavy-based pan (preferably non-stick) and heat gently while you stir. When almost at boiling point, reduce the heat and continue stirring for another 2 minutes. Add flavouring from the following list.

Onion Sauce

Peel 2 medium onions. Put each on to a skewer and boil for about 30 minutes, until soft all the way through (the skewers are helpful with this). Drain in a sieve and chop on a board, as finely as you can. Stir into the white sauce. Season to taste. Serve with lamb.

Egg Sauce

Hard-boil an egg. Peel and chop very finely on a board. Stir into the white sauce, season with salt and fine pepper. Excellent with white fish.

Parsley Sauce

Chop enough parsley as fine as sawdust to make 1 heaped table-spoon. Stir into the white sauce. Serve with vegetables or fish.

Cheese Sauce

Make the white sauce but use an extra level tablespoon dried milk. When the sauce is made, stir in 1 teaspoon made French mustard and 1 heaped tablespoon grated tasty cheddar cheese. Stir until it has melted. Serve with white fish. See also Cauliflower Cheese, p. 122.

Tomato Sauce

Add 1 tablespoon (or more) of tomato purée. Taste. If it seems sour, correct with a pinch or two of sugar. Serve with fish or vegetarian savoury cakes.

Mushroom Sauce

Finely chop 2oz (50g) mushrooms. Fry in a little soft margarine or sunflower oil for 3 or 4 minutes. Season to taste. Serve with fish.

Cucumber and Lemon Sauce

Cut 10 thin slices of cucumber and chop them on a board. Put into a mini-chopper and reduce to a purée. Add to the basic white sauce with the finely grated rind of ¼ lemon. Serve with white fish or salmon (hot).

Asparagus Sauce

Poach the tips and 1in (2.5cm) of the spears from 6 to 8 spears of fresh asparagus in water until tender. Drain and chop on a board. Put into a mini-chopper with 2 tablespoons of basic white sauce. Purée and add to remaining white sauce. Season to taste. Serve with hot salmon or salmon savoury cakes.

Béchamel Sauce (makes about ½pt (300ml)

1 level tablespoon margarine or
  butter
2 level tablespoons plain flour
  (white)

½pt (300ml) hot milk heated with
  1 small bay leaf (optional)
salt and fine pepper
2 pinches grated nutmeg

Method: Melt the margarine gently in a small non-stick pan. Stir in the flour and cook for 1 minute. Take the pan off the heat and gradually stir in the milk. Put back over the heat and cook while you stir until the sauce thickens. Season to taste with salt, pepper and nutmeg.

NOTE: If stubborn lumps develop, put the sauce into a liquidiser and blend. If any survive this, put the sauce through a fine mesh sieve.

Tomato and Herb Sauce (2–3 servings)
For the herbs use freshly, finely chopped basil, oregano or parsley.

1lb (450g) fresh tomatoes
1 tablespoon extra virgin olive or
  sunflower oil
1 clove garlic, peeled
½ teaspoon sugar

salt and finely ground black
  pepper to taste
1 tablespoon chopped herb of
  your choice

Method: Peel tomatoes, quarter and remove pips (see p. 40). Chop the flesh coarsely. Put the oil into a pan. Crush in the garlic and stir-fry for a minute. Add the prepared tomatoes, sugar and seasoning. Cook over a medium heat until the sauce has thickened, stirring from time to time. Allow to cool a little then blend in a liquidiser, adding the herb of your choice. Serve hot with fish or savoury cakes.

SAUCES FOR PASTA

What better to complement the bland taste of plain pasta than a really tasty sauce. With the problem of soft pasta sorted out (see chapter 4) here is a selection of sauces to go with it.

Salsa di Carne (Meat Sauce) (2 servings)

1 heaped teaspoon soft margarine
1 slice lean back bacon, chopped
  into tiny squares
½ medium onion, finely grated
1 small carrot, finely grated
½ stick celery, finely chopped
6oz (160g) lean, finely minced
  beef

1 tablespoon plain flour
2 tablespoons cold water
1 tablespoon dark soy sauce
¼pt (150ml) hot water
2 teaspoons tomato purée
salt and finely ground black
  pepper
2 pinches grated nutmeg

* Put sirloin steak through the mincer twice.

Method: Melt the margarine in a small saucepan. Put in the bacon, onion, carrot and celery. Gently fry while you stir for about 4 minutes. Add the beef and fry with the vegetables, turning the mixture over to brown the meat.

When the pink has turned to brown, sprinkle in the flour, mixed with 2 tablespoons cold water, and cook for 2 minutes. Add the soy sauce, hot water and tomato purée. Stir well and bring to the boil. Lower the heat and simmer with the lid on for 10 minutes, stirring from time to time. Season to taste with salt, pepper and nutmeg. Serve with hot pasta and a sprinkle of finely grated parmesan cheese.

Bolognese Sauce (2 servings)

Real Bolognese sauce is rather rich and includes liver, wine and cream. This version is plainer but more easily digested. The description 'Bolognese' has come to mean a tasty beef and tomato sauce to serve with pasta.

1 tablespoon extra virgin olive oil

1 slice lean back bacon, cut into tiny squares (optional)

½ medium onion, finely chopped

4oz (100g) finely minced lean beef

1 small carrot, finely grated

2–3 teaspoons soy sauce

1 small can peeled plum tomatoes, cut up in the tin with kitchen scissors

1 teacup water

1 tablespoon tomato purée

1 heaped teaspoon flour mixed with a little water

salt and finely ground black pepper to taste

nutmeg to taste, 1–3 pinches

Method: Put the oil into a saucepan and heat. Put in the bacon squares and onion. Stir-fry gently for about 5 minutes. Add the beef and turn it over while you fry until it has turned from pink to brown. Put in the grated carrot, soy sauce, tomatoes, teacup of water and tomato purée. Stir well. Bring to the boil, then lower heat and simmer for 10 to 15 minutes, stirring occasionally. Stir in the flour and water and bring back to the boil. Stir for 30 seconds then take off the heat and season to taste with salt, pepper and nutmeg. Serve hot with pasta, sprinkled with finely grated parmesan cheese, or use for lasagne.

Variations: To the finished sauce add 1 crushed clove garlic and/or 10 leaves fresh basil finely chopped, or, 1 teaspoon freeze-dried basil.

Tomato Sauce (makes ½pt (300ml))

Use with tiny pasta noodles or tiny squares.

1 clove garlic, peeled and put through a crusher
1 medium onion, finely chopped
1 medium carrot, grated
1 stick celery, finely chopped
1 medium can peeled plum tomatoes

1 teaspoon sugar
2 teaspoons tomato purée
salt and finely ground pepper to taste
6 leaves fresh basil, finely chopped (optional)

Method: Put all ingredients into a saucepan, except the basil. Cut up the tomatoes with kitchen scissors, bring to the boil and simmer for about 25 minutes with the pan lid off. Blend in a liquidiser and return to pan. Stir in the basil if using.

Serve hot with soft options pasta and a sprinkle of finely grated parmesan cheese or tasty cheddar for a simple dish. Serve with a soft options side salad or puréed broccoli or spinach.

Tuna and Tomato Sauce (1 serving)

small can tuna fish in oil
½ clove garlic, peeled
6oz (160g) fresh tomatoes (peeled and seeds removed), chopped

1 tablespoon finely chopped parsley
2½fl oz (70ml) water
2 tablespoons soy sauce
salt and finely ground black pepper

Method: Open the can of tuna and drain the oil into a pan. Crush in the garlic and stir-fry for a minute. Put in the tomatoes and parsley. Flake, then mash the tuna with a fork. Add to the tomato mixture. Pour in the water and soy sauce. Stir and simmer for 5 minutes. Season to taste and mix into hot soft options pasta.

GOOD GRAVY

Many people have forgotten what good gravy is, or, sadly, they have never had any, knowing only gravy stock cubes or gravy powder. Yet it is simple to make with ingredients to hand—fresh vegetable strainings, soy sauce (which is a bean stock) and meat juices if there are any.

Method One: For gravy to go with roast meat or poultry, strain off the juices from the roasting tin into a gravy separator. The fat will be lighter than the meat juices and will rise to the top. Use the spout connected to the bottom to pour out the meat juices as required.

Sprinkle the empty roasting tin with a little plain flour (fine grade). Rub the tin all over with the back of a wooden spoon to release any remaining meat juices. Pour in the vegetable strainings you have saved, heat and stir. Add the meat juices from the gravy separator and soy sauce to taste. Bring to the boil, stirring briskly, turn down the heat and simmer for a minute. Pour into a jug (or gravy boat) through a fine mesh sieve to remove any lumps. Taste and correct soy sauce if required.

Method Two: Use this method when there are no meat juices. Put two teaspoons cornflour into a cup with 2 tablespoons cold water and mix well. Pour into a pan with vegetable strainings and 2 teaspoons or more of soy sauce. Bring to the boil while you stir. Simmer for 2 minutes. A teaspoon of tomato purée will not only add flavour but turn the gravy a rich colour. Finely chopped herbs as appropriate can be added to expand the flavour. Serve with vegetarian or meat savoury cakes.

Gravy Cubes
If you have made too much good gravy and cannot bear to throw it away, cool and pour into an ice cube tray. Freeze and use as required.

Homemade Vegetable Stock Cubes
These are very easy to make. Cook a saucepanful, cool and pour into an ice cube tray. Freeze. Use by the cube as required.

Method: Chop up an onion and fry in a little sunflower oil. Prepare and chop a selection of the following vegetables: carrot, swede, turnip, celeriac, celery, green beans, cabbage, broccoli, peppers, leeks (avoid potatoes, sprouts, cauliflower and tomato). Add to onion with enough water to cover and the same amount again. Bring to the boil with the lid on, then simmer, leaving the lid off slightly. After half an hour strain through a fine mesh sieve, pressing the vegetables with the back of a wooden spoon to squeeze out the stock. Discard, saving the liquid. Season to taste with soy sauce, salt and pepper. A handful of chopped parsley added to the chopped vegetables always improves the flavour.

SALAD DRESSINGS

Although mayonnaise is not considered suitable for people who are ill, pregnant, frail or elderly because it contains raw egg yolks, other types of dressing are perfectly suitable, less rich and egg yolk free.

As the fresh juices of the raw vegetables and fruit in soft options salads are released during the processing action, little dressing is needed to moisten them. This means a small amount should be used to bring out the taste rather than moisten for chewing. The following can be used in a variety of dressings.

Oils: olive (extra virgin grade)
        sunflower or safflower
Vinegars: white wine, raspberry, balsamic, cider

You will probably find that ordinary dressings are too sharp for soft options salads, especially classic vinaigrettes (oil and vinegar). Combining them with the processed salad ingredient will bring out the sharpness and emphasise it. The sensible idea is to add a little sugar to the dressing.

   Make these dressings by putting the ingredients into a screw-top jar, closing the lid firmly. Shake well to combine and use immediately or it will settle out into two layers. If making a quantity for future use you should shake well each time you come to use it.

Vinaigrettes
Use white wine vinegar, not red.

Plain Vinaigrette
2 tablespoons sunflower oil, 1 tablespoon wine vinegar, 1 teaspoon caster sugar.

Lemon Vinaigrette
2 tablespoons sunflower oil, 1 tablespoon fresh lemon juice, 1 teaspoon caster sugar.

Vinaigrette with Mustard
2 tablespoons sunflower oil, 1 tablespoon wine vinegar, 1 teaspoon made French mustard.

Vinaigrette with Balsamic Vinegar
2 tablespoons sunflower oil, 1 scant tablespoon wine vinegar, 5 drops balsamic vinegar.

Vinaigrette with Garlic
2 tablespoons sunflower oil, 1 tablespoon wine vinegar, 1 small clove garlic, crushed through a garlic press.

Vinaigrette with onion
2 tablespoons sunflower oil, 1 tablespoon wine vinegar, ¼ small peeled onion, very finely chopped.

Vinaigrette with Olive Oil
1 tablespoon extra virgin olive oil, 1 tablespoon sunflower oil, 1 tablespoon wine vinegar.

Vinaigrette with Cider Vinegar
2 tablespoons sunflower oil, 1 scant tablespoon cider vinegar, 1 teaspoon caster sugar.

Vinaigrette with Raspberry Vinegar
2 tablespoons sunflower oil, 1 scant tablespoon wine vinegar, 6 drops raspberry vinegar, 1 tablespoon caster sugar.

Cooked Mayonnaise

¼pt (150ml) milk	2 teaspoons sugar
2½fl oz (70ml) vinegar	1 teaspoon salt
2 egg yolks	1 slightly heaped teaspoon made
2 teaspoons sunflower oil	mustard

Method: Put the mustard, oil and sugar into a basin. Mix well. In a second basin, beat the egg yolks and add to the oil mixture. Beat in the vinegar, then the milk. Stand the basin in a pan of boiling water (the water should come halfway up the outside of the basin). Heat gently while you stir until the mayonnaise has the consistency of custard. Pour into a jar. Allow to cool. Cover and store in the fridge. Use within 5 days.

Mayonnaise with Cooked Egg Yolks

1 tablespoon cooked egg yolk (hard-boiled)	½ teaspoon made mustard
2 tablespoons sunflower oil	3 pinches salt
1 tablespoon vinegar	3 pinches pepper

Method: Rub the egg yolk through a fine mesh sieve. Mix with the salt, pepper and mustard. Stir in the oil. Gradually incorporate the vinegar, stirring all the time.

Egg-free Mayonnaise

1 tablespoon soya flour	5fl oz (150ml) sunflower oil
3 tablespoons water	

Method: Put the soya flour into a small basin. Add a little of the water and mix to a paste. Gradually add the rest of the water, mix well, then whisk in the oil, drop by drop to start, then 1 teaspoon at a time until it has all been whisked in.

CHAPTER 7

Soups and Starters

Soup is a versatile food. Use it as a starter, a snack, a warming drink in a mug or a liquid main meal. It can be clear and light, thick and robust or something in between; from palest cream to darkest green, red, brown, yellow, gold or orange, with a delicate flavour or one that nearly knocks you over. And it is all soup: comforting, nourishing and entertaining. Civilisation has probably been enjoying it since the cooking pot was invented; now we have the liquidiser there is no stopping!

Soup provides a golden opportunity for putting vegetables into the daily diet, especially green ones, and as the cooking liquid becomes part of the dish, no valuable nutrients are wasted. Avoiding stale or pre-cooked leftovers and using only the best, fresh ingredients will ensure really good homemade soup, far superior to anything commercially made.

The recipes that follow are mainly for vegetable soups, although meat, fish and pulses appear as well. I have used only one kind of bought stock and that is soy sauce, a simple stock made by fermenting soya beans. I find this less overwhelming than stock cubes which contain a host of ingredients, not all of them wholesome. Soy sauce will combine well with any flavour and saves a cupboard full of varied flavours of stock cubes. It is also a great deal cheaper.

There are several points to consider about making soups. They must be tasty with a good, obvious flavour; they should be colourful (unless made with dull-coloured ingredients which will respond to a colourful garnish); and they should be so good as to be memorable. This is not such a tall order as you would imagine as good soup is very easy to make.

First, consider the accompaniments to soup—sippets, pasta, rice, little dumplings, rolls or bread, cheese, cheese straws and herbs.

Sippets or croûtons. Make in the usual way by shallow-frying cubes of crustless bread in hot sunflower oil. Turn them over as they brown. Let them cool and drain on kitchen paper. Make into crumbs in a coffee grinder and sprinkle them over the top of the soup. These sippet crumbs are excellent with pea, lentil, or split pea soup.

Little dumplings. Usually dumplings for soup are small but 'bite-sized'. By making them even smaller, if you have the time and patience, you solve that problem and they will take less time to cook. See p. 68 for the recipe.

Cheese straws. These can be made in the usual way and, when cooled, made into crumbs in an electric coffee grinder. Sprinkle generously into soup just before serving. Good with celery soup. See p. 99 for recipe.

Rice. Cooked rice can be chopped even smaller on a chopping board using a large-bladed, sharp knife.

Rolls and bread. Can be made into crumbs and sprinkled into soups. Break into pieces, including the crusts, and put into an electric coffee grinder. Even French bread will succumb, and although the texture is lost, the all-important taste is not.

Crumbs can be fried in a little soft margarine to make a soft-textured sippet/croûton substitute. Serve in a small bowl with a teaspoon.

Pasta. There are special tiny pastas for soups or you can make your own from vermicelli (see pp. 62–66). Use in clear soups.

Cheese. Finely grated tasty cheddar or cheshire cheese can be sprinkled lightly into soup just before serving. Avoid too much as it tends to make clumps.

Herbs. Favourites for soup are finely snipped chives (use scissors and hold the chives over the soup), parsley, finely chopped, and fresh basil, torn into tiny pieces (needs patience!).

VEGETABLE SOUPS

Apart from frozen peas and canned tomatoes, the main ingredients in the following soups are fresh vegetables. Some of the soups will be unfamiliar to you, but remember there is no gap of days, months or even years before the making and serving of homemade soups. It is more likely to be a few minutes, or at most an hour or two, so more flavours are possible.

All recipes are for *2 servings*. When frying the onion in the oil, make sure it is done gently so as not to turn the onion brown. Always taste your soups and adjust the stock (soy sauce) and seasonings before serving.

Fresh Tomato Soup
A delicately flavoured soup to serve either hot or chilled. Use tomatoes with a good flavour. Organic or homegrown are best. Use a medium-sized saucepan.

½ medium onion, finely chopped	1 to 1½ teaspoons soy sauce
small knob margarine	caster sugar, salt and fine pepper
3 medium-sized, fresh tomatoes, chopped	1 heaped teaspoon finely chopped fresh parsley
½pt (300ml) water	

Method: Fry the onion for 3 minutes in the margarine. Add the tomatoes and about half the water to the pan. Stir and pour into a liquidiser goblet. Put in the soy sauce and blend. Put a fine mesh sieve over the pan. Pour the liquid through it to remove the pips. Add the remaining water and bring to the boil. Lower heat and simmer for 3 minutes. Taste. Add a pinch or two of sugar if it tastes sour. Season to taste and stir in the parsley. (If serving cold, add extra sugar as it will lose its sweetness a little when chilled.)

Tomato Soup
A cheerful, orange-coloured soup which uses inexpensive canned tomatoes.

¼ medium onion, finely chopped	½pt (300ml) water
2 teaspoons sunflower oil	caster sugar, salt and fine pepper
1 small (or ½ medium) can peeled plum tomatoes	1 heaped teaspoon finely chopped fresh parsley
1 teaspoon soy sauce	

Method: Fry the onion for 3 minutes in the oil. Put into a liquidiser goblet with the tomatoes and half the water. Blend and return to the pan through a fine mesh sieve. Add the remaining water, soy sauce and a pinch of sugar. Bring to the boil and simmer for 2 minutes. Taste and season. Stir in the parsley and serve hot. Good with fried soft breadcrumbs or grated cheese sprinkled on.

Tomato and Basil Soup
Make as for tomato soup but instead of the parsley stir in 2 or 3 leaves of fresh basil torn or cut into tiny pieces.

Cream of Tomato Soup
Make as for tomato soup but stir in 2 tablespoons single cream, heated (but not boiled) gently. The cream must be about the same temperature as the soup or it will curdle. Omit parsley if you wish.

Pepper and Tomato Soup

A soup that improves with standing. Tasty and highly nutritious.

¼ medium onion, sliced thinly
2 teaspoons sunflower oil
½ clove garlic, peeled and put through a garlic press
1 medium-sized red or green pepper, de-seeded and chopped into small pieces
3 canned peeled plum tomatoes, chopped
¼ teaspoon sugar
2 teaspoons soy sauce
½pt (300ml) water
salt and fine black pepper
1 heaped teaspoon finely chopped parsley

Method: Fry the onion in the oil for 3 minutes while you stir. Crush in the garlic, put in the pepper, tomatoes, sugar, soy sauce and about half the water. Bring to the boil then simmer for 5 minutes. Add the remaining water and blend. Return to the pan through a fine mesh sieve. Stir in the parsley, taste and season. Serve hot. If you feel the soup is too thin, stir in 2 level teaspoons cornflour mixed with 1 tablespoon cold water. Bring to the boil and simmer for 2 minutes while you stir.

Mushroom Soup

Canned or packet mushroom soup generally looks and tastes like beige custard. Homemade mushroom soup is never the same twice. Button mushrooms will produce a delicate flavour with an almost pale pink colour. The open kind of mushrooms with dark gills turn into a dark, almost black soup with a robust flavour to match, and give new meaning to the description 'full-bodied'.

¼ medium onion, finely chopped
2 teaspoons soft margarine
2oz (50g) mushrooms, chopped
8fl oz (225ml) water
1 heaped teaspoon low-fat dried milk granules
1½ teaspoons soy sauce
salt and fine black pepper

Method: Fry the onion in the margarine for 2 minutes. Put in the mushrooms and about half the water. Bring to the boil and simmer for 5 minutes. Mix the milk into the remaining water and add to the pan. Pour into a liquidiser goblet, blend and return to the pan. Add the soy sauce, stir and taste. Season and serve hot. Top with fried breadcrumbs if you wish. Sprinkle over the soup just before serving, about 1 tablespoon per bowl.

Cream of Mushroom Soup

Make as for mushroom but add 2 tablespoons single cream before blending.

Celery Soup

This is one of a few soups that improve with standing. A few hours will allow the flavour to develop nicely. Green celery makes the best soup and the celery seeds will bring out the flavour.

½ medium onion, finely chopped	1½ teaspoons soy sauce
2 teaspoons butter	good pinch of celery seeds
2 or 3 sticks of celery, including	salt and fine pepper
leaves, finely sliced	celery leaves for garnish
¼pt (150ml) water	(optional)

Method: Fry the onion for 2 minutes in the butter. Add the celery and stir-fry for 2 minutes. Pour in the water and bring to the boil. Lower the heat and simmer for 8 to 10 minutes or until the celery is tender. Allow to cool a little, then blend in a liquidiser. Strain back into the pan through a fine mesh sieve, pressing with the back of a wooden spoon to release all the juices. Put in the soy sauce, stir, taste and season. Sprinkle in the celery seeds and leave to stand (optional). Reheat. Pour the soup into bowls and place a celery leaf in the centre of each bowl.

Cream of Celery Soup

Make as for celery soup but add 2 teaspoons of cornflour mixed with 2 tablespoons cold water and 2 tablespoons single cream, when you reheat. Bring *almost* to the boil, then simmer while you stir for 2 minutes. The soup will be thick and creamy.

Celery and Celeriac Soup

Make as for celery soup but use 1½ sticks celery and a piece of peeled celeriac about the size of ½ a medium potato, chopped into small pieces. You may need a little more water. Makes a creamy, thick soup without adding cream or a thickener.

Cheese Straws for Soup

Roll out a small piece of leftover pastry. Spread one half lightly with French mustard. Sprinkle with finely grated tasty cheddar cheese. Put the other piece of pastry on top and go over it with a rolling-pin to press the two pieces together. Cut with a sharp knife into fingers and place on a greased baking sheet. Bake at the top of the oven at Gas 7/220°C/425°F for about 10 to 12 minutes. Do not let them brown. Cool, break into pieces and either chop very small or make into crumbs for sprinkling on soup

Carrot Soup

¼ medium onion, finely chopped
2 teaspoons butter
2 medium-sized carrots, sliced
   thinly
8fl oz (225ml) water
½ stick celery, finely sliced

1 teaspoon soy sauce
caster sugar, salt and fine black
   pepper
1 teaspoon finely chopped
   parsley or coriander

Method: Fry the onion gently in the butter. Add the carrot slices. Stir-fry for a minute, then add most of the water followed by the celery. Bring to the boil, then turn down the heat and simmer for 15 minutes or until carrot is tender. Add the remaining water and pour into a liquidiser goblet. Blend and return to pan. Add the soy sauce. Taste and add seasoning. If it tastes too sweet, add a few drops of lemon juice. If it is not sweet enough, add sugar by the pinch until correct. Sprinkle in the parsley and serve hot.

NOTE: For a quicker soup, coarsely grate the carrots and finely chop the celery. This will only need 8 to 10 minutes instead of 15 or longer.

Watercress Soups

The watercress should have dark green, glossy leaves and be free of minute snails. Wash well in a large bowl of cold water. Watercress is very nutritious and is rich in iron. Use both the leaves and stems for soup.

Thick Watercress Soup

¼ medium onion, finely chopped
2 teaspoons soft margarine
½pt (300ml) water
½ medium-sized potato, grated
   coarsely

½ bunch or packet of watercress,
   chopped coarsely
1½ teaspoons soy sauce

99

Method: Fry the onion in the margarine for 3 minutes. Add about half the water to the pan, put in the grated potato and bring to the boil. Simmer for about 10 minutes with the lid on. Take off the heat and add the remaining water. Stir and pour into a liquidiser goblet. Put in the watercress and soy sauce. Blend, pour back into the pan and bring to the boil. Simmer for 5 minutes, season to taste and serve hot. Can also be served chilled from the fridge in hot weather.

Thin Watercress Soup
A dark green, strong-tasting soup.

¼ medium onion, finely chopped
2 teaspoons sunflower oil
¾ bunch or packet of watercress, coarsely chopped

8fl oz (225ml) water
1 teaspoon soy sauce
salt

Method: Fry the onion in the oil for 3 minutes. Put the cooked onion, the watercress and water into a liquidiser goblet. Blend and return to the pan. Add the soy sauce, bring to the boil. Turn down the heat and simmer for 5 minutes. Season. Serve hot, or chilled from the fridge in hot weather.

Leek and Potato Soup

2 teaspoons soft margarine
¼ medium onion, finely chopped
8fl oz (225ml) water
1 medium-sized leek, trimmed, cleaned and cut into thin slices

2 teaspoons soy sauce
1 medium-sized potato, peeled and thinly sliced
salt and fine pepper

Method: Melt the margarine in a saucepan. Fry the onion gently for 2 minutes. Add the leek and mix with the onion, continuing to fry for a minute. Add most of the water, the potato and soy sauce. Bring to the boil, then simmer for about 10 to 15 minutes, until the leek is tender and the potato soft. Pour in the remaining water and transfer to the liquidiser goblet. Cover the goblet with a tea towel as the soup may splash out. Blend and return to pan. Taste and season. Serve hot.

Vichyssoise
Make as for leek and potato soup but prepare 2 leeks using only the white parts. When the soup is made, leave it to grow cold. Chill in the fridge for an hour. Stir in 2 tablespoons single cream. Serve

sprinkled with finely chopped chives. A classic summer soup for warm weather.

Vegetable Broth

This is a good soup to give people who are feeling poorly. It is nothing much to look at but is high in potassium and has a more delicate flavour than thick vegetable soup. You will need a medium-sized pan.

½ medium onion, sliced thinly
2 teaspoons sunflower oil
mixed fresh vegetables, diced or chopped to fill ⅓ of a medium-sized pan
water
2 teaspoons soy sauce

salt and fine black pepper
1 tablespoon chopped cooked rice or tiny pasta noodles (see pp. 62–66)
1 heaped teaspoon finely chopped parsley or fresh herbs

Method: Fry the onion in the oil for 3 or 4 minutes. Put in the prepared vegetables and half fill the pan with water. Bring to the boil and put the lid on slightly to one side. Simmer for 20–25 minutes, until all the vegetables are soft. Strain into a basin through a fine mesh sieve. Press lightly with the back of a wooden spoon to squeeze the vegetables, then discard. Put the liquid back into the pan. Add the soy sauce. Sprinkle in the parsley and tiny noodles. Bring to the boil and simmer for 2 minutes. Taste and season. Serve hot.

NOTE: Suitable vegetables for the mixture are carrots, swede, turnip, green beans, celery, green and red peppers, broccoli, lettuce, cucumber and celeriac.

Minestrone Soup

A robust soup with a good selection of vegetables. Make the tiny pieces of vermicelli yourself. Helpings are generous.

¾ medium-sized onion, chopped
2 teaspoons extra virgin olive oil
1 clove garlic, peeled and put through a garlic press
3 canned tomatoes, put through a fine sieve
¾pt (450ml) water
2 teaspoons soy sauce
1 level teaspoon tomato purée
1 small carrot, diced

½ stick celery, chopped
2 small, tender cabbage leaves, torn into pieces
2 level tablespoons canned haricot beans (drained)
1 pinch celery seeds
1oz (25g) tiny (uncooked) vermicelli pieces—see p. 64
fine black pepper
1 tablespoon finely chopped parsley

101

Method: Fry the onion gently in the oil for 4 minutes and take the pan off the heat. Crush in the garlic and mix well. Put in the tomatoes, water, soy sauce, tomato purée, carrot, celery and cabbage. Stir and add the beans and celery seeds. Bring to the boil and put on the lid, slightly to one side to let out the steam. Turn down the heat to simmer for 25 minutes. Put through a mouli on the coarsest plate and return to the pan. Put in the vermicelli, bring back to the boil and simmer for 2 or 3 minutes. Stir in the parsley. Season with pepper and serve hot.

Thick Vegetable Soup
If you are buying vegetables in season, then your vegetable soup will vary from month to month. Compare this with tinned or packet vegetable soup which is the same whatever the month.

As the method for making is the same for each one, here it is, followed by a few suggestions. The liquidiser will give you a smooth texture, the mouli a coarser one.

Method: In a medium-sized saucepan fry the onion in the oil for 3 minutes, stirring from time to time. Add the other vegetables and about ¾ of the water. Bring to the boil and simmer with the lid on for 15 to 20 minutes. Take off the heat, add remaining water and soy sauce and put into a liquidiser goblet or put through a mouli on the coarse plate. Return to pan and heat through. Taste and season, diluting with water if it turns out too thick. Serve hot. A tablespoon of single cream will make it into Cream of Vegetable Soup.

Vegetable selections

Winter

½ medium onion, sliced
2 teaspoons sunflower oil
½ medium carrot, sliced
½ small parsnip, sliced
½ small turnip, sliced

2 Brussels sprouts, sliced
½ medium potato, sliced
½pt (300ml) water
1½ teaspoons soy sauce
salt and fine black pepper

Spring

½ medium onion, sliced
2 teaspoons sunflower oil
6 spinach leaves, chopped
about 8 cauliflower florets,
   sliced

½ medium carrot, sliced
1 small leek, sliced
½pt (300ml) water
1½ teaspoons soy sauce
salt and fine black pepper

Summer

3 spring onions, trimmed and
  chopped
2 teaspoons soft margarine
½ courgette
2 baby carrots, sliced
1 tablespoon peas

1 small new potato, sliced
2 button mushrooms
½pt (300ml) water
2 teaspoons soy sauce
salt and fine black pepper

Autumn

½ medium onion, sliced
2 teaspoons sunflower oil
1 stick celery, chopped
1 teaspoon tomato purée
½ medium carrot, sliced

4 string beans, chopped
½pt (300ml) water
2 teaspoons soy sauce
salt and fine black pepper

Vegetables for mixed vegetable soups

*onion	*cauliflower	courgette
*carrot	fennel	mushroom
*celery	*broccoli	potato
*swede	*Brussels sprouts	lettuce
*turnip	*cabbage	leek
celeriac	spring greens	spring onions
green beans	tomatoes	*asparagus

Generally speaking, onion plus four other vegetables makes a good
balance. Try to let one vegetable dominate to give the soup character.
The vegetables marked * are not recommended for vacuum flasks
as they respond badly to being kept hot for a long time. If you have
made a particularly good soup, write down the ingredients so that
you can make it another time.

Clear Onion Soup

A clear soup which needs something at the bottom of the bowl to
give interest. Use tiny pasta shapes or chopped, cooked rice. An
ideal hot drink for people with a cold.

2 medium onions, thinly sliced
½ clove garlic, put through a
  garlic press
¾ tablespoon sunflower oil
¾pt (450ml) water
2 teaspoons soy sauce

pinch of sugar
salt and fine black pepper
1 heaped teaspoon finely
  chopped parsley
1 tablespoon suitable tiny pasta
  (see pp.62–66)

Method: Fry the onion in the oil for about 5 minutes, stirring frequently. Crush in the garlic. Add the water and soy sauce and bring to the boil. Put the saucepan lid on, slightly to one side, and simmer gently for 20 minutes. Strain into a basin through a fine mesh sieve. Discard the onion. Return the clear liquid to the pan and put in the pasta. Bring to the boil again and simmer for 2 more minutes. Sprinkle in the parsley and serve.

Cucumber Soup
A refreshing cold soup for a hot summer's day.

¼ cucumber, peeled and chopped
½ carton natural flavour yoghurt
chilled milk to thin down

2 mint leaves, finely chopped
salt and fine pepper

Method: Put the cucumber into a liquidiser goblet with the yoghurt. Blend. Thin down with chilled milk. Stir in the mint, taste and season. Serve chilled from the fridge with a thin slice of cucumber floating in the centre.

SOUPS WITH PULSES

Lentils, beans and peas make robust soups that are filling and ideally suited for winter. An overnight soak in a bowl of water for dried lentils and split peas will ensure the minimum cooking time.

Lentil Soup

2½oz (65g) lentils
1 medium onion, coarsely
  chopped
1 tablespoon sunflower oil

½ medium potato, sliced thinly
2 teaspoons soy sauce
½pt (300ml) water
salt and fine black pepper to taste

Method: Wash the lentils in a fine mesh sieve. Pick them over for any discoloured ones or pieces of grit. Leave overnight in a bowl of water to swell. Drain in a colander before using for soup. Put all ingredients into a medium-sized saucepan and bring to the boil. Turn down the heat and simmer for about 35 minutes, giving it a stir from time to time and adding a little more water if it starts to get too dry. Take off the heat and allow to cool a little before blending in a liquidiser. Taste and season. Reheat and serve. Croûton crumbs or fried soft breadcrumbs can be sprinkled over the top before serving.

Split Pea Soup

Make as for lentil soup but use 4oz (100g) split peas instead of lentils and a medium-sized carrot, sliced, instead of the potato.

NOTE: Some people with a weak digestion may not be able to cope with either lentil or split pea soup.

Baked Bean Soup

This is a soup for baked bean fans. Fry 1 heaped teaspoon of finely grated onion in 2 teaspoons of soft margarine for 3 minutes. Put into a liquidiser goblet with a small tin of baked beans and 1 teaspoon soy sauce. Blend and pour into pan. If it is too thick, thin down with a little water. Serve with a little dish of fried soft breadcrumbs to sprinkle on the top.

FISH AND MEAT SOUPS

Fish Soup

This high protein soup from Italy is often served as a main meal.

12oz (350g) mixed fish (see note below)

1½ tablespoons extra virgin olive oil

1 heaped teaspoon finely chopped onion

½ clove garlic, peeled and put through a garlic press

1 teaspoon finely chopped parsley

1 small can peeled plum tomatoes, finely sieved

1 walnut, powdered to a paste with a pestle and mortar

1 tablespoon white wine

½ small bay leaf

salt and fine black pepper

soft bread, crusts cut off to serve

Method: Clean and pick over the fish of your choice, removing any bones. Cut into very small pieces. Use a large saucepan to fry the onion in the oil for a minute, adding the parsley and crushing in the garlic. Add the puréed tomato, walnut, wine, fish, bay leaf and seasoning. Bring to the boil and cook steadily for 3 or 4 minutes or until the fish is tender. Take out and discard the bay leaf. Serve hot with the soft bread.

Fish

Make up the 12oz (350g) with whatever is going—cod, plaice, haddock, mackerel, canned sardines and tuna, prawns. Prawns will need to be chopped finely. A mussel or two will also need fine chopping. Avoid calamari as it is rather tough.

NOTE: If tomato pips are not a problem add the canned tomatoes just chopped.

Chicken Soup

about 6oz (160g) raw chicken
   pieces, sliced
¾pt (450ml) water
1 small carrot, sliced
1 small onion, sliced
½ stick celery, chopped

½ teaspoon tomato purée
1 small bay leaf
3 teaspoons soy sauce
salt and fine black pepper to taste
1 teaspoon finely chopped
   parsley

Method: Put the chicken pieces into a large saucepan with the water. Slowly bring to the boil (take off any scum with a spoon). Add the vegetables, purée, bay leaf and soy sauce and put the lid on the pan. Bring to the boil and simmer for about 30 minutes. Allow to cool a little, discard bay leaf, then blend in a liquidiser to make a smooth soup. Season to taste. Strain through a fine mesh sieve and serve hot with the parsley stirred in at the last moment.

STARTERS

Just the tempting food to get the appetite stimulated and the digestive juices flowing. Simplest of all are melon or grapefruit finely chopped and served with a teaspoon. Sweeten with caster sugar if necessary. Fruit or vegetable juices are also suitable (see chapter 5) and any of the following.

Avocado and Orange (2 servings)

1 ripe avocado
1 sweet orange
2 teaspoons vinaigrette

2 pinches caster sugar
salt and fine pepper to taste

Method: Have ready 2 avocado dishes. Peel the orange. Chop the flesh finely, saving the juice. Cut the avocado in half lengthways and remove the large stone. Spoon out the avocado flesh and mash on a plate, using a fork. Put the empty skins into the avocado dishes. Pour the orange juice over the mashed avocado and work it in. Mix the vinaigrette in a cup with the sugar and seasoning to taste. Put alternate spoonfuls of the avocado mixture and the chopped orange in the avocado skins. Pour over the dressing and serve as soon as possible with tiny squares of soft bread, with the crusts cut off and spread with soft margarine or butter. Put the dishes on to small plates with teaspoons and the bread squares round the edges.

Variation: Add ½ teaspoon sesame seed oil to the dressing.

NOTE: The orange juice will stop the avocado turning brown.

Pawpaw with Prawns (2 servings)

1 ripe pawpaw
2 heaped tablespoons defrosted
  prawns
2 tablespoons mayonnaise

fine pepper to taste
3 pinches sugar
squeeze of fresh lemon juice

Method: Cut the pawpaw in half lengthways. Scoop out and discard·
the black seeds. Cut a small slice from the back of each half so that
they won't fall over. Spoon out the flesh and mash on a plate with
a fork. Put back into the skins and make a well in the centre of each
one. Rinse the prawns under the cold tap. Shake dry and chop on a
board as finely as you can. Put into a small basin with the mayonnaise, sugar, lemon juice and pepper to taste. Spoon it into the centre
of each pawpaw half and build into a mound. Serve with small
squares of soft bread and butter.

Variation: Use crabmeat instead of prawns.

Pesto (serves 1)
A modest list of ingredients can be turned into a wonderfully
flavoured starter. See chapter 4 for the pasta.

½ portion hot, drained cooked
  pasta (tiny squares or fine tiny
  noodles)
½oz (15g) fresh basil leaves,
  chopped
pinch salt
sprinkle of finely ground black
  pepper
½ clove garlic, peeled and finely
  chopped

1 heaped teaspoon pine nuts
  (optional)
2 tablespoons extra virgin olive
  oil
½oz (15g) grated Parmesan
  cheese
small knob butter

Method: Put the basil, garlic, pine nuts and cheese into a mortar and
pound with a pestle until you have a green paste. Work in the salt,
pepper and oil, a little at a time. Put the knob of butter into the pan
with the cooked pasta and toss. Add the green sauce and toss again.
Serve immediately.

Chicken Liver Pâté

8oz (225g) chicken livers
1 small onion, chopped finely
1 tablespoon soft margarine
½ clove garlic, peeled and put
  through a garlic press

1 pinch dried mixed herbs or ¼
  teaspoon finely chopped fresh
salt and fine pepper to taste
1½ tablespoons milk
1 teaspoon sherry (optional)
2 teaspoons soy sauce

Method: Wash the livers and pick them over. Discard any stringy or yellow parts. Chop finely. Use a small pan to fry the onion in the margarine for about 4 minutes, while you stir. Crush in the garlic then put in the liver, herbs and seasoning. Stir-fry, using a wooden spoon to crumble the livers as they cook. After 4 or 5 minutes they should have changed to a greyish colour and be crumbly. Allow to cool and put into a liquidiser with the milk, sherry and soy sauce. Blend. Return to the pan and heat again while you stir to make a thick paste. Stir in sherry. Spoon into a small dish and allow to cool. Use on soft, crustless bread, spread thickly and cut into small squares.

NOTE: If used, the sherry makes this recipe unsuitable for anyone on an alcohol ban due to medication.

Prawn Cocktail (1 serving)

Unsuitable for serving in a showy glass. Instead use a ramekin dish as it processes down to quite a small amount. Serve with a teaspoon and tiny squares of soft bread, crusts cut off, and soft margarine or butter.

1 heaped tablespoon defrosted
  prawns or shrimps, the
  smaller the better
1 tablespoon mayonnaise (see
  pp. 24 and 92)
3 lettuce leaves from a non-bitter
  lettuce, torn into small pieces

5 slices thin, coarsely chopped
  cucumber
2 tomatoes, peeled, de-seeded
  and finely chopped with a
  pinch of sugar
salt and fine pepper

Method: Rinse the prawns well in cold water. Drain and chop finely on a board. Put the mayonnaise into a cup. Add the prawns and stir well. Put the lettuce leaves into a mini-chopper with the cucumber. Process to a light purée. Season to taste. Put into the ramekin. Fold (don't mix) in the tomato. Pile the prawn mixture in the centre and serve as suggested above.

See also p. 122 for Leeks in Cheese Sauce, and chapter 9 for pizzas. All these can be served in small portions as a starter.

CHAPTER 8

Salads, Vegetables and Vegetarian Dishes

With five vegetables to eat per day, this chapter is important. Salad vegetables processed to a coarse purée will delight with their brilliant colours and surprisingly intense flavours. Cooked vegetables will satisfy and sustain as a vital food—alas, usually abandoned on a non-chew regime. A selection of vegetarian-based dishes has been included, but more are to be found in chapters 5 and 9.

SALADS

Be prepared for surprises. The very nature of salad makes it unsuitable for those who must avoid chewing, so your culinary efforts are required to thwart nature. The results can be nutritionally and visually spectacular—jewel-bright colours, from cyclamen pink and brilliant greens to sparkling yellow and dazzling reds and oranges. Here are amazing salads to nourish all year round, the greatest variety being available during the winter months, as you will see. Although a mini-chopper (miniature food processor) is the key to making soft option salads, most ingredients need to be grated, chopped or prepared in some way *before* processing to achieve the desired texture. The following table shows lists of available and suitable ingredients. Although some might appear to be unlikely candidates, they can indeed be made into salads suitable for eating with specially prepared

109

high protein food—cheese, cold chicken, hard-boiled eggs, ham, prawns, salmon (canned or fresh), sardines or tuna (canned), ground cashews or almonds. Fresh crab or lobster for luxury meals can also be added to the list.

Salad ingredients

raw crisp/ crunchy	raw soft	cooked	herbs	dried fruit
* apples * beetroot ♦ cabbage, shredded red/white/ green * carrot * celeriac * celery ♦ cress ♦ onion * parsnip ♦ peppers * radish ♦ spinach, shredded young leaves ♦ spring onion * swede * turnip ♦ watercress	♦ avocado ♦ banana ♦ grapes, seedless * courgette ♦ cucumber ♦ lettuce, shredded ♦ orange segments ♦ tomato, peeled and de-seeded	♦ beetroot ♦ green beans ♦ leeks peas ♦ potatoes rice	chives, snipped garlic (put through a garlic press) ♦ parsley	apricots sultanas prunes, stoned raisins, seedless

Prepare fruit and vegetables in the usual way, washing/trimming/peeling etc.
Before putting into the mini food-processor:
ingredients marked * should be finely grated
ingredients marked ♦ should be coarsely chopped.
See p. 40 for special preparation of tomatoes.

Preparation of Salad, Fruit and Vegetables for a Mini-food Processor

Wash everything before preparation.

Apples—choose sweet eating apples. Avoid extra-sour varieties such as Granny Smith. Grate finely.
Apricots—soak in water for a few hours. Drain in a colander and chop into small pieces.

Avocado—peel, halve and remove and discard central stone. Slice, then chop; it will discolour so prepare at the last minute.

Banana—peel and cut into thick slices.

Beetroot (cooked)—peel and slice, chop coarsely.

Beetroot (raw)—cut off top and bottom. Peel and slice. Grate finely. Needs care as it colours everything pink.

Cabbage (crisp)—cut out a section. Remove and discard outer leaves. Chop as small as you can by hand.

Carrot—trim, peel and grate finely. It will turn brown unless used quickly.

Celeriac—cut out a section, peel and grate finely.

Celery—pull off a stalk, trim, slice and cut into small pieces.

Chives—hold in a bundle and snip with kitchen scissors or put on a board and cut with a sharp knife.

Courgette—trim off stalk and bottom, slice thinly, chop.

Cress—cut off with a pair of kitchen scissors, at the bottom of the stems. Chop.

Cucumber—can be indigestible for some people. Leave the skin on, cut into slices and chop.

Garlic—peel and put through a garlic press. For just a hint of this flavour, rub a cut clove around the bottom of the processor goblet.

Grapes—seedless are easiest. If you do want to use ones with seeds in, cut the grapes in half and winkle out the pips with the tip of a teaspoon. Chop coarsely.

Green beans (cooked)—chop coarsely.

Leeks (cooked)—chop coarsely.

Lettuce—avoid bitter varieties and the white stems at the base of leaves which are often bitter. Roll up leaves and slice, then chop. Some of the more decorative types on sale are wasted in the food processor. English crisp, cos, little gem (if not bitter) and round lettuce are the most useful. Iceberg tends to be watery and tasteless after processing.

Onion—trim off top and bottom. Peel away and discard the brown papery skin. Slice and chop.

Orange—peel the fruit and cut into thin slices, then chop. Remove any pips.

Parsley—this can be very coarse and extremely tough, so choose young leaves, discarding the stems. Chop on a board using a sharp knife.

Parsnip—as for carrot.

Peas—raw or cooked can be left as they are.

Peppers—cut out and discard stem and seeds. Slice and finely chop.

111

Potatoes—new potatoes can be cooked in their skins, cooled and then peeled easily. The skins will be tough even after cooking and are difficult to process. Old potatoes should be peeled before cooking. Chop both kinds coarsely.

Prunes—cut out the stones if they are not already pitted. Soak for an hour, drain and chop.

Radish—trim off leaves and long root. Slice thinly then chop.

Raisins—as for sultanas.

Rice—should be slightly overcooked to render it soft. It tends to be too sticky for the processor and is best chopped on a board using a large, sharp knife.

Spinach—use only young, tender leaves. Roll up and shred with a sharp knife. Chop shreds into shorter lengths.

Spring onions—trim off roots and the coarsest part of the green leaves. Slice and chop.

Sultanas—soak in water for an hour to plump up. Drain and chop on a board.

Swede—cut out a wedge. Peel and cut into thin slices, chop.

Tomato—peel and de-seed as described on p.40. Cut out the pale green part where the stem was attached. Chop coarsely.

Turnip—cut off top and bottom. Peel and cut into small wedges. Chop.

Watercress—this must be thoroughly washed and inspected, then washed again under the cold tap. (Watch out for tiny snails which can cause liver fluke). Chop coarsely.

Problem fruit and vegetables for soft options:

Cauliflower and Brussels sprouts—these smell really unappetising if processed:

Pears—disintegrate to liquid and have very little taste.

Black olives—need to be used in very small quantities and tend to blacken any mixture. If you have the patience to stone 2 or 3 and then chop really small, they can be used as a garnish.

Processing salads

There is much more to the processing and presentation of salads than putting the ingredients into the machine, switching on and spooning the result into a soup bowl. First, combinations are important for taste, colour and moistness, and second, while too many ingredients are confusing, too few can be boring. Choice of dressing can make or mar a soft options salad. If serving with fish or shellfish,

Soft Options Bread

One of the joys of life – homebaked bread, soft textured, crusts removed. A melt-in-the-mouth, essential daily food.

Soft Options Vegetables

Fresh vegetables for juice, soup, a colourful terrine of purées and bold garnishes.

Soft Options Fruit

Fresh fruit for juices, homemade fruit yoghurt
and puréed fruit salad.

Soft Options Treats

A slice of celebration sponge with cream and fruit purée,
delicate snow dessert and miniature soft chocolates.

a lemon vinaigrette is preferable. With meat a mustard vinaigrette will balance the flavour, and so on.

If your salad turns out too moist (or even watery) it can be strained in a fine mesh sieve. Too dry a salad will not go through the processor enough to reduce the mixture to non-chew consistency.

There are several very moist salad vegetables which can be used to produce a nicely moist mixture. Tomato, cucumber and lettuce all fall into this category. Mixed salads with more than three ingredients become confused for flavour, so here are a few basic combinations that never fail. They all need processing to purée in a mini-chopper. See detailed guidance above. Amounts are for one serving.

Green Salad
2 kinds non-bitter lettuce, about 3 leaves of each, torn into pieces, 8 thin slices cucumber, white of 1 spring onion, vinaigrette with mustard or raspberry vinegar (1 teaspoon).

Purple Salad
1 small beetroot, either raw (finely grated) or cooked, 1 tomato, ⅛ red pepper, 1 teaspoon vinaigrette.

Red Salad
⅛ red pepper, 1 small carrot, ½ small cooked beetroot, 1 teaspoon vinaigrette, 8 thin slices cucumber, green skin cut off.

Pink Salad
2 raw button mushrooms, 4 red radishes, 1 heaped tablespoon white cabbage, small piece of cooked beetroot for colouring, 1 teaspoon vinaigrette, 1 tomato.

Orange Salad
2 drained canned apricot halves, 1 small carrot, ½ orange, peeled, 1 teaspoon vinaigrette with lemon.

Dark Green Salad
Few young and tender spinach leaves, 2 cos lettuce leaves, handful of watercress, 1 teaspoon vinaigrette with garlic.

Pale Green Salad
¼ stick celery (green) or 10 thin slices courgette with the skin left on, heart of a round lettuce, 8 thin slices cucumber, ¼ peeled apple, 1 teaspoon vinaigrette with lemon.

Yellow Salad
1 yellow lettuce heart, ⅛ yellow pepper, ¼ eating apple, peeled, 3 orange segments, vinaigrette with lemon.

You will doubtless want to try combinations of your own. Keep a note of the really successful ones in a notebook. Avoid over-dressing salads. Soft options salads require much less dressing than an ordinary salad.

COOKED VEGETABLES

'Greens' of some kind should be eaten every day. Whatever the season greens are always available—Brussels sprouts, sprout tops, spring greens, green cabbage, spinach and kale. Those with the darkest colour are the best value nutritionally. Really fresh greens will squeak when squeezed. It is a common practice in supermarkets to keep vegetables back until the price goes up. The small green-grocer wouldn't dare sell wilty greens and will be pleased to show them off to you, crisp and squeaky.

To prepare greens for soft options needs, use a sharp vegetable knife and cut away coarse leaves, thick stalks, bruised or discoloured leaves and anything which looks in poor condition. Wash in lots of cold water. Inspect closely for anything living which enjoys greens—aphids, caterpillars, slugs and snails. Look out for grit and earth which are best cleaned off under the running cold tap. Spinach is particularly prone to dirt and may need extra washing and picking over. Trim a slice off the base of every Brussels sprout and cut a cross into it to ensure even cooking. Cabbage can be cut into wedges or very coarsely chopped or shredded.

Method: Put about an inch of cold water in a saucepan and bring to the boil. Put in the prepared greens and poke down with a wooden spoon. Bring to the boil again and put on the lid. Lower the heat but cook steadily for 7–10 minutes, checking after 5 minutes to see if the water needs topping up—don't let them boil dry. Continue cooking until greens are tender and a knife will cut easily through them. Spinach will cook in a few minutes but kale will take up to 30 minutes if tough. Sprouts, cabbage, spring greens, etc., will take from 15 to 25 minutes on average. Strain in a colander. Put into a mini-chopper with a little of the straining water and process to a purée. Put into a fine mesh sieve to drain a little more and serve as

114

soon as possible. Save all the strainings for soup or gravy as they should contain valuable nutrients.

Broccoli
Really counts as 'greens'. Wash and cut into large florets or spears. Cook in a little water with the lid on for 7 to 10 minutes. If just using the florets they can be chopped finely on a board. If using the stems as well, use a mini-chopper. Process to a purée with some of the straining water. Strain in a fine sieve. Serve as soon as possible.

Leeks
One medium-sized leek makes a portion. Trim off the tops where the leaves start to look coarse and cut off the roots. Split lengthways and open out under the cold tap to wash out any grit or earth. Chop into short lengths and cook in a little boiling water with the lid on the pan. Top up if they start to look dry. Young leeks will take about 10 minutes but older, tougher kinds will take up to 25 minutes. Test with the point of a knife to see when they are tender. Purée in a mini-chopper with a little of the straining water. Put into a fine mesh sieve and strain. Save the strainings for gravy or soup.

Serve hot with cheese sauce or white sauce (see chapter 6), or with a small knob of butter or soft margarine.

French Beans, String Beans
Just top and tail, and chop into short lengths. Put into a pan with enough boiling water to come halfway up the beans. Bring to the boil again and cook for 7–10 minutes, with the lid on, until tender. Purée in a mini-chopper with a little straining water. Strain in a fine mesh sieve. Save the strainings for gravy or soup. Serve hot.

Runner Beans, Stick Beans
Wash well then trim off the tops, bottoms and side strings, using a very sharp knife. Any bean which feels tough, discard. Slice through the pods at an angle, cutting through the little beans inside. Cook and serve as for French beans—10–15 minutes for young, tender beans and up to 25 minutes for older, tougher beans.

Peas
As these are more likely to be the frozen kind, put into a pan with enough water to cover and bring to the boil. Lower the heat and simmer for 3 or 4 minutes. Strain them, purée in a mini-chopper

with a little of the straining water. Strain in a fine mesh sieve. Garden peas have a higher nutritional value than petit pois.

Onions

A much neglected vegetable and an ideal one for soft options. Buy ones which feel hard, with dry, papery skins (any sign of softness means they have started to rot). Trim off the top and bottom (roots). Take off the layers of skin until the onion is white, crisp and shiny.

Boiled

Select smallish onions of a similar size. Prepare and thread through the centres (top to bottom) on skewers. Put into a pan of boiling water and simmer for about 30 minutes. Serve chopped finely with white, parsley or cheese sauce (see chapter 6).

Fried

Chop onions finely on a board, using a large chopping knife. Put about 1 tablespoon of sunflower oil, extra virgin olive oil or soft margarine into a frying-pan or shallow saucepan. Fry gently while you stir for 2 minutes. Drain off most of the fat and continue cooking for another 2 minutes. A very tasty vegetable.

Mushrooms

Wash well under the cold tap. Slice, then chop very finely on a board, using a large chopping knife. Cook in very little sunflower oil just to get them started, using a frying-pan or shallow saucepan. After about 3 minutes strain off the fat. Serve hot with fried bread-crumbs or on their own. Overcooking will cause mushrooms to become rubbery so just cook until softened.

Cauliflower

Prepare and cook as for broccoli.

Broad Beans

Use new season beans which will be the tenderest. You will need about 2lb (1kg) to produce enough beans for 2 servings. Shell then boil the beans in water until tender. If young, 15 minutes will be enough, but older beans will take up to 25 minutes. Drain in a colander and allow to cool a little. Cut open the tough outer skins (discard) and take out the soft green insides. Mash on a plate using a small fork. Put into the oven to heat up again. Serve with a small knob of butter on top.

POTATOES

This versatile vegetable can be fried, roasted, baked or boiled. Several varieties are available and there is a distinct difference between new crop and old potatoes that have been stored for months. The skins are tough, even after cooking, so for soft options they are always peeled. The middle responds brilliantly to the potato masher or an ordinary fork and the resulting texture is delightful. There is a subtle difference between varieties as regards flavour and the method used for cooking also provides different flavours for each variety.

Some have been developed for their mashing abilities—King Edwards and Cara are two—others for keeping, for frying, baking or roasting, or just for some novelty such as red skins or an oval shape. Potatoes grown in southern Europe tend to be smaller, yellow, waxy in appearance and stronger in flavour than British-grown. Wet climates are excellent for the large, softer-textured potatoes, ideal for chips, roasting and mashing. There seems to be an all-year-round supply of new potatoes coming in from countries such as Cyprus and Egypt to supplement a later new potato season here. From being a humble, everyday vegetable the potato has reached 'designer' status and price, with some varieties new or resurrected! With variety well known to be the spice of life, this is all good news for soft options cuisine, as the potato is an important feature of the main meal of the day.

There is really no problem with the centre of the potato but the outside does need attention. Even after peeling, some methods of cooking will cause a tough 'skin' to form on the outside. This means a second peeling after cooking or some other way of sorting out the problem.

New Potatoes

When the crop is young the potatoes are usually small with a strong thin, papery skin. If you have the time and patience to peel them they don't taste as good as those boiled in their skins and your efforts will have been wasted. The problem is to remove the skins after boiling, while the potatoes are hot.

Some will respond to the masher, allowing you to pick out the pieces of skin. After mashing in the saucepan, spread the potato out on a plate. Trawl backwards and forwards with an ordinary fork to find the skins and remove them. Put the middles back in the pan and mash again, adding a small knob of butter and a little boiling

117

water. Heat through while you stir. Serve sprinkled with a little finely chopped parsley (optional).

You will need double the usual amount of potatoes as it is a wasteful procedure. However, the result is the inimitable taste of new potatoes. Best-flavoured of all are Jersey Royals although they are inclined to be firm even after cooking. Select the larger-sized ones if you can.

Depending on variety and size, boil new potatoes in their skins for 15 to 20 minutes. The water should cover the potatoes in the pan. Cook with the lid slightly to one side to let out some of the steam.

Old Potatoes

These can be peeled and boiled, roasted or fried or baked in their skins. Peel off the skin and cut out any eyes or discoloured parts. Cut into thick slices. Cook potatoes in enough water to cover. Put the lid on the pan slightly to one side. Bring to the boil. Cook steadily for 15–20 minutes until soft.

Drain in a colander. Put the potatoes back into the pan and add a small knob of soft margarine or butter, salt and fine pepper to taste and a pinch or two of nutmeg. Mash until smooth, then add a little milk and beat in with a wooden spoon. If you still have the odd lump, press through a fine mesh sieve with the back of a wooden spoon. Take care not to overbeat or the potato will become heavy and sticky. Serve hot, forked up to give it texture. Cold mashed potato can be fried in a little hot sunflower oil, turning once. Avoid frying it to the crisp stage, keeping it soft.

(The commercial version of mashed potato comes dry, in a packet. It bears little resemblance to the fresh version and is used mainly by institutions. Ingredients are not the same as for homemade mashed potato. The best mashing potato with a lovely floury texture is King Edwards variety.)

Roast Potatoes

Use a double portion to achieve 1 serving. For best results roast potatoes in the minimum of fat, using sunflower oil. Peel and cut into large chunks. Grease a baking tin with oil. Sprinkle the potatoes with a few drops (only) of sunflower oil. Pick up each chunk and smooth over the oil. Put back in the tin. Wipe your hands with kitchen paper and put the tin on the top shelf of the oven, preheated at Gas 7/220°C/425°F. Roast for about 35–45 minutes.

Spear each chunk with a fork. Put it on a board and trim off the outer roast 'skin' with a sharp knife. Mash what is left on a plate, using a fork. Put back in the bottom of the oven until required. This tastes completely different from mashed boiled potato.

Baked Jacket Potatoes

Use fairly large or medium-sized potatoes. Scrub and cut out any eyes or discoloured parts. Prick all over with a fork to stop them bursting. Stick a metal skewer longways through each one and put on a baking sheet. Bake for an hour in a preheated oven at Gas 7/ 220°C/425°F. When soft inside, remove skewers and cut the potato. in half. Hold in a clean folded tea towel while you scoop out the flesh with a spoon. Using a fork, mash on a plate with a little butter or soft margarine. Serve hot.

Chips

There are two ways of cooking chips. The high-fat way is to fry them in hot oil. The low-fat way is to bake them in the oven. Either way they are a problem as crispness is part of their character.

Fried—peel old potatoes and cut into long slices, then across to make chips. Try to get them all the same thickness. Fry in a pan of hot sunflower oil. Drain in a fine mesh sieve.
Baked—prepare oven chips in the same way as for fried. Place on a lightly oiled baking tray. Sprinkle with a few drops of sunflower oil and turn the chips over by hand to coat them lightly with the oil. Wipe your hands on kitchen paper. Put the chips into a preheated oven, Gas 7/220°C/425°F, on the top shelf and bake for 25 minutes.

The method of serving both kinds of chips is the same. Trim off any parts which are obviously too crisp. Put into a warm dish and cover with greaseproof paper. Keep warm in the oven for about 10 minutes until no longer crisp. Put on a board and chop into thin slices. Chop again to make smaller pieces. Serve immediately.

Fried Potato

Boiled potato is not the only potato for frying. The insides of jacket potato, roast potatoes or mashed potato can all be fried and will all taste quite different in a subtle way. Heat a little sunflower oil, soft margarine or butter in a pan. Have ready the potato, mashed with a fork, and fry lightly for 2 minutes, then turn over with a spatula and fry on the other side for 1 minute. Serve hot. It will keep warm in the oven for up to 10 minutes.

ROOT VEGETABLES

Carrots, Turnips, Swede, Parsnips and Celeriac

These are all prepared and cooked in the same way. Wash or scrub, peel and trim. Cut into small chunks or thick slices. Cook as for boiled potatoes, allowing up to 25 or 30 minutes depending on how old the vegetables are. Young vegetables should only need about 15 to 20 minutes. If cooking more than one, cook in the same pan. After draining in a colander, mash with a potato masher. Season to taste with salt and fine pepper and put in a small knob of butter or soft margarine. If they turn out too stiff, add a dash of boiling water. Finely chopped parsley can be added if desired.

Mixtures which include potato as a base are always tasty and an attractive colour. Cook the root vegetable for 10 minutes before putting in the potato slices. Here are some combinations.

potato, carrots and swede
potato and celeriac
potato and parsnips with a few drops of lemon juice
swede and carrot
carrots and turnip

All the root vegetables are good on their own. If they are still lumpy after mashing, press through a fine sieve with the back of a wooden spoon and discard the lumps.

Parsnips can be roasted in the same way as potatoes, then peeled and mashed.

Vegetable Terrine

For some reason stripes always look attractive. An eye-catching selection of vegetable purées can be pressed firmly into a small loaf tin then turned out and cut into thick slices with a large, sharp knife. First line the loaf tin with film for ease of turning out. Vegetable purées to use are: finely chopped spinach, puréed peas, mashed potato, carrots, swede, turnip, parsnip and celeriac. Contrast the stripes by putting the brightly coloured vegetables between the paler ones for maximum effect.

The vegetables should not be too wet or the layers will not hold their shape. Spinach should be put into a fine mesh sieve after chopping and pressed with the back of a wooden spoon to remove excess water. Always serve with a gravy or sauce to replace the moisture. Slices can be wrapped individually and frozen for later use.

Defrost and either reheat in a covered dish in the oven, microwave or put between two plates over a saucepan of boiling water. Serve with an egg or cheese dish.

See the colour illustrations for a typical vegetable terrine using potato, spinach, carrot and swede.

STIR-FRY VEGETABLES

This is a quick cooking method for a mixture of vegetables which are intended to be lightly cooked, served in their own gravy or the juices plus a little soy sauce. The vegetables are prepared and thinly sliced to be cooked not separately, but as a mix. This way of cooking cannot be faulted for nutritional value and it means only one pan to wash up. The pan should have rounded or sloping sides.

Always start with the finely chopped white of a spring onion, lightly fried for a few seconds in a tablespoon of sunflower oil. Have your other vegetables prepared (see below) and put them into the pan in order of hardness—root vegetables first, semi-hard vegetables such as peppers, celery, broccoli and tender greens second and soft vegetables such as mushrooms and cucumber last. Use the centre of the pan to turn over the vegetables as they cook quickly, adding a little water to stop them catching. A large portion will only take a few minutes to cook. The heat needs to be quite high.

For soft options, vegetables can be finely sliced and then finely chopped before putting into the pan. (Carrots are best avoided as they are so hard.) Spinach is best put in as whole leaves, taken out and chopped on a board before putting back in. When cooking has finished, put in 1 or 2 teaspoons of soy sauce to combine with the juices to make a tasty gravy. If you would prefer more and thicker gravy put in 2 tablespoons of water mixed with 1 teaspoon of corn-flour plus the soy sauce.

Here are three combinations, all making one serving:

A white of 2 spring onions, 1 mushroom, 1 medium potato, handful of spinach leaves (young and tender).

B white of 2 spring onions, chunk of celeriac the size of a small potato, 1 stalk celery, ¼ of a red pepper.

C white of 2 spring onions, 10 broccoli florets, chunk of swede the size of a small potato, 2 or 3 tender cabbage or spring green leaves.

Serve these with fried fish or a Chinese dish.

Bubble and Squeak (1 serving)

1 portion boiled potato
1 portion cooked greens

1 tablespoon sunflower oil
salt and fine pepper to taste

Method: Chop both the potato and cabbage as finely as you can. Heat the oil in a frying-pan and put in the two vegetables. Fold together and fry lightly for 4 minutes. Turn over with a fish slice and cook on the other side. Serve hot with cold meat slices and smooth chutney (see chapters 9 and 14). A good Monday dinner.

VEGETARIAN DISHES

Cauliflower Cheese (2 servings)

Cook 8oz (225g) cauliflower florets until tender. Drain and chop very finely on a board, using a large chopping knife. Put into 2 small warmed ovenproof dishes. Cover with cheese sauce (see p. 86) and sprinkle with soft breadcrumbs. Bake for 5 minutes at Gas 7/220°C/425°F, top shelf, and serve with soft bread and butter, cut into small squares.

Leeks in Cheese Sauce (1 serving)

Prepare and cook 1 leek. Drain and chop finely on a board. Grease a small pie dish and put in the leek. Top with a finely chopped hard-boiled egg. Cover with cheese sauce (see p. 86) and bake in a hot oven Gas 7/220°C/425°F for about 8 minutes. Serve hot with tiny squares of soft bread and butter, crusts cut off, or mashed potato.

NOTE: This recipe will also make 2 starters in ramekins. Omit mashed potato. Bake only for 5 minutes. Serve on a saucer with a teaspoon and about 6 tiny squares of bread and butter.

Leek and Potato Pie (1 serving)

Grease a small pie-dish. Prepare ½ a medium leek and slice finely. Peel and thinly slice an old parboiled potato. Finely grate 1oz (25g) tasty cheddar cheese. Crack an egg into a cup and whisk with a fork. Make your pastry (see chapter 4). Fill the pie-dish with a layer of potato, a layer of leek, and a sprinkle of cheese. Repeat. Put on a pastry rim first. Brush with water and cover with a large piece. Trim off all round with a knife. Press the edge lightly on to the pastry rim (do not flute). Cut a hole in the centre and pour in the egg. Bake in a preheated oven as suggested for the pastry of your choice. Do not overbake. If you are worried the pastry will be too crisp, cover the pie with a sheet of greaseproof paper.

NOTE: Can be served hot or cold. The pastry may need to be removed, made into crumbs by chopping on a board with a large knife and sprinkled back on the pie (see p. 38). The filling should respond to mashing with a fork as it is eaten but can be removed, chopped finely and put back into the dish.

Eggs Florentine (1 serving)

1 portion cooked fresh spinach, puréed and well drained	1 soft-boiled or poached egg* 1 portion cheese sauce (see p. 86)

Method: Put the spinach on a warmed plate. Use a spoon to shape into a 'nest'. Chop the egg finely. Put a spoonful of cheese sauce into the spinach nest. Top with the chopped egg. Cover both egg and spinach with the remaining cheese sauce. Serve hot with small squares of soft crustless bread and soft margarine or mashed potato.

All-in-one TVP Dinner (2 servings)
This is a vegetarian version of the All-in-one Beef Dinner.

1 heaped tablespoon natural flavour TVP	2 medium old potatoes, peeled and quartered
½ medium onion, finely chopped	1 teaspoon cornflour
1 tablespoon sunflower oil	1 tablespoon water
2 medium carrots, sliced thickly	3 pinches dried mixed herbs or 1 teaspoon fresh, finely chopped
2oz (50g) mushrooms, halved	¼ small cabbage cut into 2
2–3 teaspoons soy sauce	wedges or prepared spring
salt and fine pepper to taste	greens

Method: Reduce TVP to powder in a coffee grinder. Fry the onion in the oil for about 2 minutes. Take off the heat and put in the powdered TVP, the prepared vegetables, soy sauce and seasoning. Pour in enough water to cover. Give it a stir and put your choice of greens on top and either simmer on the hob for about 25 minutes with the lid partly on, or bake in the oven in a covered casserole for 45–50 minutes at Gas 6/200°C/400°F. If it begins to dry out add more boiling water. After cooking, remove the vegetables and thicken the liquid in the pan with the cornflour mixed with 1 tablespoon cold water. Stir in and heat through on the hob, adding the herbs. Finish cooking. Process and serve as suggested on p. 132.

NOTE: There is no need to blend the gravy as the TVP is put in as
* Hard-boiled egg if soft egg is not allowed.

a powder. Extra vegetables to put in are chunks of peeled celeriac and swede, chopped green beans and chopped red or green peppers.

Quick Vegetarian Dinner
Make vegetable soup. Stir in 1 heaped tablespoon natural flavour TVP made into powder (use a coffee grinder). Reheat, adding a little water if it is too thick. Cook while you stir for a minute. Taste and adjust soy sauce and seasoning. Serve with 'dumplings' of mashed potato on top. Serve hot. See chapter 7 for vegetable soups.

Variation: Add chopped mixed herbs or just one herb.

See also: TVP pie (p. 136), Savoury Cakes (pp. 140–1), Vegetarian Style Curry (pp. 143–4), Egg Curry (p. 144).

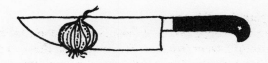

CHAPTER 9

Main Meals

Although this is the most important meal of the day, it is the one where the non-chewer most often comes to grief, and frequently in public. All too often the food is left on the plate. So here is a wealth of options to nourish, satisfy and make the chewers around you envious. Do eat plenty of vegetables with the meals as they are an important part of the daily diet.

FISH DISHES

Ideally, buy skinned and boned fillets of fish. Wash each fillet under the cold tap and run your fingers over the fish, searching for any bones that have been left in. As they will be firmly embedded, cut them out with kitchen scissors. Time spent doing this extra preparation is never wasted.

Baked Fish (2 servings)

Cod, haddock, plaice, sole and salmon fillets, preferably skinned as well as boned, are all suitable for baking. Allow 4 to 5oz (100–130g) fish per serving. Wash the fish under the cold tap and prepare as described above. Pat the fillets dry with kitchen paper. Grease a shallow ovenproof dish and place the fillets in it. Squeeze over the juice of ½ a lemon. Dot the tops of the fish with a little soft margarine or butter. Put a piece of greaseproof over the top of the dish and bake in a preheated oven at Gas 4/180°C/350°F for 15 to 20 minutes depending on the thickness of the fish. Serve with one of the sauces from chapter 6 and with puréed vegetables—carrots, spinach, broccoli, peas and mashed potato.

Poached Fish (1 serving)

Place a fillet of fish (see below) in a small frying-pan. Add enough liquid (see below) to cover the fish. Bring to the boil, then simmer for 10 minutes or until cooked and starting to flake. Lift out with a fish slice and put on a warmed plate. Flake and mash the fish and serve with mashed potato, puréed vegetables—peas, spinach, broccoli, green beans, carrots—and (with white fish) puréed, peeled plum tomatoes.* Season to taste.

1 Cod, haddock or plaice and milk and water.
2 Salmon and water with 1 tablespoon white wine plus a tablespoon of freshly chopped parsley.

NOTE: A sauce can also be served with poached fish. With white fish serve egg, parsley, cheese, tomato or cucumber and lemon sauce. With poached salmon serve asparagus, parsley or cucumber and lemon sauce. (See chapter 6 for recipes.)

Fried Fish in Breadcrumbs (2 servings)

To avoid frying for too long, making the fish too crisp, it is fried in thin slices instead of thick pieces. Best oil for frying is sunflower oil. Plaice is already a thin fillet and does not need cutting in half.

2 fillets white fish—cod or haddock for slicing, plaice as it is
plain flour
1 egg, beaten on a plate

2 slices soft bread made into crumbs and put on a plate
oil for frying

Method: Wash the fish and inspect for bones. Put on a board and, with a sharp knife, cut in half lengthways to make thin fillets. Dab dry with kitchen paper. Sprinkle with flour on each side, dip in the egg and roll in the breadcrumbs. Fry in hot shallow oil for 3 to 5 minutes, turning once. Serve on warm plates with mashed potato and puréed peas, spinach or broccoli. Also serve a sauce, for example tomato (see pp. 86 and 89).

* Canned—put through a fine mesh sieve if necessary.

Quick Fish Pie (1 serving)
Poach a fillet of cod or haddock in milk. Drain, flake and mash. Put into a small pie-dish. Cover with 3 tablespoons cheese sauce. Top with mashed potato. Serve with puréed peas and carrots.

PIZZAS AND PASTAS

Pizza (2 main meal servings or 4 smaller pizzas)
Serve this versatile dish as a main meal, a starter or a snack. The crisp edging which anchors the topping will have to be discarded, but the centre is soft and can be cut into tiny squares. The toppings can be varied and must be chopped or grated very finely before they are sprinkled on.

6oz (160g) plain white flour
¼oz (7g) instant/Easyblend yeast
1 pinch sugar
3 pinches salt
1 tablespoon sunflower oil
lukewarm water
1 tablespoon extra virgin olive oil (optional)

1 medium can tomatoes drained and blended in a liquidiser to a purée
toppings (see list below)
2 tablespoons finely grated parmesan cheese

Preheat oven: Gas 8/230°C/450°F. *Position*: top shelf and next one down. *Baking time*: About 12 minutes.

Method: Put the flour and yeast into a warm bowl with the sugar and salt. Mix well. Drizzle in the sunflower oil. Add enough water to make a soft dough. Cut in half with a knife. Roll out each one into a circle the size of a dinner plate using more flour. Grease 2 baking sheets and put the circles on them, using the rolling-pin to lift them. Turn over the edge like a hem, all the way round. Spread with the tomato purée. Sprinkle with your choice of topping and the parmesan cheese. Bake. After 5 minutes switch the baking trays round and finish baking. Have ready 2 warm serving plates. With a pair of kitchen scissors, cut off the 'hem' crust, leaving the pizzas on the hot baking sheets and taking care not to burn yourself. Wait another 2 or 3 minutes for the bases to soften, then cut into sections. Put each one on a board and, using a large chopping knife, cut into very thin strips and then across to make tiny squares. Use a spatula to transfer to the warmed serving plates, as you cut up the wedges. (The more finely you can cut them up the easier they will be to eat.)

Either use ham, mushrooms, peppers or courgettes on their own or with a herb, or combine toppings.

Toppings

Finely chopped lean ham, 1 slice
½ courgette, finely grated and chopped
2 medium-sized mushrooms, finely chopped
Finely chopped cooked leek, 2 heaped tablespoons
Very finely chopped red or green pepper (de-seeded)
4 leaves fresh basil, chopped finely
A few fresh oregano leaves, chopped finely
1 clove garlic, put through a garlic crusher

Combinations

Leek and potato (both cooked)
Ham and mushroom with garlic
Pepper, courgette, garlic and basil or oregano
Ham and cooked leek

NOTES: Do not give people garlic unless they are fans. If you would prefer to use tasty cheddar instead of parmesan, grate 1oz (25g) very finely. Sprinkle over the pizzas as they come out of the oven and allow to melt into a soft covering. Do not bake in the oven as a tough covering will be the sad result.

Soft Lasagne (2 servings—one to eat and one to freeze)

2 servings cooked tiny pasta squares (see chapter 4) with 1 tablespoon butter or extra virgin olive oil stirred in
2 servings Bolognese Sauce (see p. 88)

⅓pt (200ml) Béchamel Sauce (see p. 87)
1 tablespoon finely grated tasty cheddar cheese for the top

Method: Grease a small ovenproof dish and a suitable freezer container. Spread a layer of Bolognese sauce over the bottom of each one; cover with a layer of pasta and then a thin layer of Béchamel sauce. Repeat the layers, finishing with Béchamel sauce. Bake the one to eat in a preheated oven Gas 6/200°C/400°F for 15—20 minutes, until bubbling. Sprinkle with the cheese and serve. When cold, seal up the remaining one and put in the freezer. Allow several hours to defrost and cook as above or microwave. Serve sprinkled with cheese.

TIP: Although it is customary to cover the top with grated cheese before baking, this will go crisp and chewy. It is better to sprinkle the cheese over the hot lasagne where it will melt to a soft consistency and not be a problem.

Soft Spaghetti Bolognese (1 serving)
Cook tiny vermicelli noodles (see p. 64). Drain in a fine mesh sieve. Return to empty pan with a small knob of soft margarine. Stir gently until melted. Put in 2 tablespoons Bolognese sauce (see p. 88). Turn over gently to distribute. Sprinkle with finely grated parmesan cheese or tasty cheddar. Serve with puréed spinach or broccoli or with a soft options salad (see chapter 8).

PROCESSING ROAST DINNERS FOR NON-CHEW MEALS

In a domestic situation it is often just one member of the family group who needs non-chew food. It may seem like the only solution but puréeing the whole dinner just for that person is a daunting prospect. The meal still needs to be presented in an attractive way, with several distinct flavours and not just one overall taste. A brownish-grey slurry will not tempt anyone and the rest of the family might be put off their own food at the sight of such a culinary disaster, albeit a deliberate one. Allow up to ten minutes to process a meal.

General advice
It is important to keep everything warm while you process the meal—the serving plate, the unprocessed and the processed food. This ensures it comes to the table at a suitable temperature for eating immediately. Use a spoon to place the processed foods on the serving plate in neat, separate mounds. Use an electric mini-chopper to reduce most foods to a thick or thin purée, as appropriate. Some will require chopping finely on a board with a large, sharp chopping knife as they are unsuitable for the mini-chopper. A few foods can be mashed with a table fork. Don't start any processing until the whole meal is ready, including gravy.

Vegetables
Purée in a mini-chopper using a tablespoon of gravy or the cooking liquid if they are too dry to make a purée on their own. Attend to the vegetables first. Roast potatoes need to be trimmed with a knife and just the insides mashed on a plate using a table fork (see p. 118 for more details).

Roast Beef and Yorkshire Pudding
After processing the vegetables, cut slices of meat off the joint. Cut into long strips on a board, trimming off any fat, skin and gristle. Cut the strips across to make small squares and put into a mini-chopper with 2 tablespoons of gravy. Reduce to a coarse purée. Put on the warm serving plate with the vegetables in a thinnish layer with a defined shape. Keep warm while you trim the crispy parts off two portions of Yorkshire pudding. Put the soft pieces on to a board and chop finely down to the size of sawdust (your knife needs to be really sharp). Put on the plate in a neat mound, partly on the meat. Pour on a little gravy and serve.

Roast Lamb with Mint Sauce
After processing the vegetables, cut pieces off the joint and put on a board. Trim off all the fat, skin and gristle. Cut the meat into small pieces, put in a mini-chopper with 1–2 tablespoons of gravy and process to a coarse purée. Put on to the warm serving plate in a thinnish layer with a defined shape. Dress the meat with 2 or 3 teaspoons of mint sauce. Serve immediately with gravy.

Roast Pork, Stuffing and Apple Sauce
After processing the vegetables, cut slices off the joint and put on a board. Trim off all the fat, gristle and skin. Cut the remaining meat into narrow strips, then across to make small squares, and process in a mini-chopper with 1–2 tablespoons gravy. Put on the serving plate with the vegetables in neat mounds and the meat in a flat, defined shape. Select any really grizzled out, dry crackling. Chop as best you can then pulverise with a pestle and mortar. Sprinkle the meat with the crackling. Put apple sauce and soft stuffing (see p. 68) next to the meat. Pour on a little gravy and serve.

NOTE: The crackling is an extremely difficult food to process. Only the taste will remain. To really grizzle out the fat, put strips of crackling under a hot grill, turning frequently.

Soft Meat Slices (1 serving)
Cold meat is a useful food to serve with soft options salad, bubble and squeak, or in sandwiches. However, its natural chewiness is something of a problem and it can look unpleasant when minced or chopped finely. This recipe allows meat to be pulverised easily in a liquidiser and then set into a large, thin slice. Ham, chicken, pork, beef, lamb, turkey and even grouse, duck, goose or pheasant can be used for the

meat. Leftovers from roasts are ideal as the meat must be pre-cooked. Flavours are intensified by the processing so the slices are tasty.

over 1½oz (40g) lean, cooked meat ¼pt (150ml) water
½oz (15g) cornflour stock or flavouring (see below)

Method: Pick over the pieces of meat, discarding any fat, gristle or skin. Make sure the lean weighs 1½oz (40g) and chop into small pieces. Put into a liquidiser goblet with cornflour and water and any stock or flavouring. Blend to a liquid and pour into a small pan. Bring to the boil and cook steadily for 2 minutes while stirring. Taste and adjust stock or flavouring. Rinse a dinner plate under the cold tap. Pour the mixture onto the plate and pick out any pieces of meat which have escaped the liquidiser blade. Leave on a wire rack for 25–30 minutes to cool and set. When cold, cut into shapes or quarters.

Eat the same day, covering the slice with food film if it is not to be eaten immediately. In hot weather serve chilled from the fridge. Lay in nearly overlapping slices to serve with special soft salads.

NOTE: Pastry cutters or a tumbler can be used to shape slices. Use the offcuts for sandwiches. The bottom of the slice will be shiny in appearance, the top will be matt. Serve them whichever way you decide is most attractive.

Flavourings
The actual flavour of the meat is much more intense in these soft slices; no chewing is required to release the taste. Extras to balance the flavour may be required. Here are a few suggestions:

Ham—¼ teaspoon (or less) of made French mustard.
Chicken—a few drops fresh lemon juice and soy sauce and a small pinch dried sage or tarragon (powdered).*
Pork—Use ½ cup non-fizzy apple juice as part of the ¼pt (150ml) water and a small pinch dried mixed herbs with a few drops soy sauce.
Beef—¼ teaspoon of made French mustard or ¼ teaspoon horseradish sauce, few drops soy sauce.
Lamb—½ teaspoon mint sauce, few drops soy sauce *or* 1 heaped teaspoon redcurrant jelly and a few drops of soy sauce, *or* pinch of powdered rosemary, a few drops of soy sauce and a cut clove of garlic rubbed over the plate.
Turkey—pinch dried mixed herbs, few drops soy sauce.
Grouse—2 teaspoons redcurrant jelly, few drops soy sauce.

* Use a pestle and mortar to reduce dried herbs to powder.

Duck—1 tablespoon apple sauce, few drops soy sauce.
Goose—1 tablespoon apple sauce, 2 pinches dried mixed herbs, few drops soy sauce.
Pheasant—2 teaspoons redcurrant jelly, few drops soy sauce.

NOTE: The lamb version needs good flavouring or it will taste too 'muttony'.

ALL-IN-ONE DINNERS

Complete soft, non-chew main meals can be made all in one with the protein as part of the gravy and a selection of vegetables including potato to mash, chop finely or put into a mini-chopper. As only one pan or casserole is used it saves a good deal of washing up!

Beef, lamb, pork, chicken or TVP (see pp. 123—4) can all be used. The processed vegetables can be served separately or just folded (not mixed) together to look colourful and appetising. No valuable nutrients are wasted and the dishes are extremely tasty.

The dinners can be cooked in two ways—quickly on the hob or more slowly in the oven.

Casserole cooking
Preheat the oven at Gas 6/200°C/400°F, bake for 45—50 minutes. (Bake with the lid on.)

Hob cooking
Simmer on the hob for about 25 minutes with the lid partly on.

Serving
To serve, whichever way the dish is cooked, remove the vegetables with a slotted spoon and put on to a warmed plate. Sort them out and either mash with a fork or potato masher, chop finely on a board, or process in a mini-chopper. Arrange in a warmed serving bowl and keep warm while you make the rich gravy. Everything left in the pan or casserole should be spooned into the liquidiser and blended.

Thickening the gravy
If it turns out too thin, put back into the pan with a teaspoon of cornflour mixed with a tablespoon of water. Heat while you stir until thickened. If it turns out too thick add a little water. Pour around or over the vegetables and serve.

If you have used several small amounts of vegetables, just pick out a colourful one to mash or chop finely and use as a garnish. The rest can be put through a coarse mouli, mashed with a potato masher or processed in a mini-chopper in two or three lots.

Blend the gravy in a liquidiser as above and serve in the same way, but with the one vegetable on top, as a garnish.

A variety of main meals follows to make 2 servings. Just halve the amounts for a single serving, or serve one and freeze one for later use.

All-in-one Beef Dinner (2 servings)

about 6oz (160g) lean sirloin steak
plain flour for coating
½ medium onion, finely chopped
1 tablespoon sunflower or extra virgin olive oil
2 medium carrots, sliced thickly
2oz (50g) mushrooms, sliced
2 medium old potatoes, peeled and quartered (or more)

2–3 teaspoons soy sauce
salt and fine black pepper to taste
hot water
¼ small cabbage, cut into 2 wedges
1 heaped teaspoon finely chopped parsley to garnish (optional)

Method: Trim any fat and gristle from the steak. Cut into cubes and coat with flour. Fry the onion in the oil for 2 minutes. Put in the meat and turn it over while you cook over a high heat just to seal it. Take the pan off the heat and add the prepared carrots, mushrooms and potatoes. Cover with hot water, stir and bring to the boil. Add the soy sauce and seasoning. Place the wedges of cabbage on top and either bake in the oven with the lid on or cook on the hob with the lid partly on. Check after 15 minutes to see if it is getting too dry. If so, top up with more (boiling) water. Finish the cooking, process and serve as suggested.

Variations: Add 1 teaspoon made French mustard with the seasoning. Add ½ clove garlic through a garlic press with the onion.

NOTE: Thicken gravy as necessary.

All-in-one Lamb Dinner (2 servings)

lean from 4 or 5 loin lamb chops
plain flour for coating
½ medium onion, finely chopped
1 tablespoon sunflower oil or

2–3 teaspoons soy sauce
salt and fine black pepper to taste
1 clove garlic, peeled
½ teaspoon dried rosemary, pow-

extra virgin olive oil
2 medium carrots, sliced thickly
1 medium turnip, peeled and
    quartered (optional)
2 medium old potatoes, peeled
    and quartered

dered in a pestle and mortar,
    or 1 teaspoon fresh, finely
    chopped
hot water
about 5oz (130g) broccoli florets

Method: Cut the meat into small pieces and coat with flour. Fry the onion in the oil for 2 minutes. Put in the meat and turn it over while you cook over a high heat, just to seal it. Take the pan off the heat and put in the carrots, turnip, potatoes, soy sauce and seasoning. Crush in the garlic and sprinkle in the rosemary. Cover with water and bring to the boil. Stir and either bake in the oven with the lid on or cook on the hob with the lid partly on. After half an hour in the oven put the broccoli florets on top, put the lid back on and finish cooking. For the hob version put the broccoli florets on top after 15 minutes. Top up both versions with boiling water if they begin to look dry. Finish cooking. Process and serve as suggested on p. 132.

NOTE: Thicken gravy if necessary.

All-in-one Pork Dinner (2 servings)

2 lean pork chops or fillets
plain flour for coating
½ medium onion, finely chopped
1 tablespoon sunflower or extra
    virgin olive oil
2 medium carrots, sliced thickly
½ medium-sized cooking apple,
    peeled, cored and sliced
    thickly

2 teaspoons soy sauce
2 fresh sage leaves, chopped
    finely, or ½ teaspoon dried
salt and fine black pepper to taste
2 medium old potatoes, peeled
    and quartered
hot water
about 12 prepared Brussels
    sprouts (see p. 114)

Method: Trim any fat and gristle off the pork. Cut into small cubes and coat with flour. Fry the onion in the oil for 2 minutes. Put in the meat and turn it over while you cook over a high heat, just to seal it. Take the pan off the heat and add the prepared carrots, apple, soy sauce, sage, seasoning, potatoes and hot water. Stir well and put the sprouts on top. Bake in the oven with the lid on or cook on the hob with the lid partly on. Top up with boiling water if it begins to get too dry. Finish cooking. Process and serve as suggested on p. 132.

Variation: To make a richer gravy add 3 canned prunes, de-stoned, to the liquidiser when you blend it.

NOTE: Thicken gravy as necessary.

All-in-one Chicken Dinner (2 servings)

2 chicken breasts, skinned
plain flour for coating
½ medium onion, finely chopped
1 tablespoon sunflower oil
1 medium leek, trimmed and cut
   into short lengths
2 medium carrots, sliced thickly
2 small mushrooms, sliced
2 medium old potatoes, peeled
   and quartered

finely grated rind of ¼ lemon
salt and fine black pepper to taste
2—3 teaspoons soy sauce
hot water
2 heaped tablespoons frozen peas
   (defrosted)
1 heaped teaspoon finely
   chopped parsley

Method: Cut the chicken into cubes and coat with flour. Fry the onion in the oil for 2 minutes. Add the chicken and turn it over while you cook over a high heat to seal it. Take the pan off the heat and add the prepared leeks, carrots, mushrooms and potatoes. Put in the lemon rind, seasoning and soy sauce. Cover with water, bring to the boil and stir. Either bake in the oven with the lid on or cook on the hob with the lid partly on. Check after 15 minutes to see if it is getting dry. If so top up with more hot water. For the last 10 minutes of cooking put in the peas. Finish cooking, process and serve as suggested on p. 132, with parsley sprinkled on. The peas should be blended in with the gravy.

NOTE: Thicken gravy if necessary.

POTATO-TOPPED PIES

Ideal for using up leftovers, these easy-to-make pies have mashed potato on top and protein and gravy or sauce underneath. An old-fashioned, tasty dish. Serve with two vegetables—broccoli, peas, carrots, swede or spinach (puréed)—for a good main meal. Can be frozen for future use.

Cottage Pie (2 servings)
Use leftovers from a joint of roast beef, or cooked, fresh minced beef.

½ medium onion, very finely
   chopped
1 tablespoon sunflower oil
2 medium-sized mushrooms,
   finely chopped

2 teaspoons soy sauce
4oz (100g) pre-cooked beef,
   minced finely
salt, fine pepper and nutmeg
8oz (225g) boiled potatoes (hot)

1 tablespoon plain flour	knob soft margarine
4 tablespoons water	2 tablespoons skimmed milk

Preheat oven: Gas 6/200°C/400°F. *Position*: top shelf. *Baking time*: 8–10 minutes.

Method: In a small saucepan, fry the onion in the oil for 2 or 3 minutes. Add the mushrooms and continue to stir-fry for another 2 minutes. Mix the flour with 2 tablespoons water until smooth, then add the remaining water and soy sauce. Put the prepared meat into the pan with the flour mixture. Heat through and stir until the gravy has thickened. Season to taste with salt and fine pepper. Turn into a greased pie-dish and keep warm. Mash the potatoes with the margarine and milk. Season to taste, adding 2 pinches nutmeg. Spoon on to the meat and spread out smoothly with a knife. Bake and serve hot with puréed vegetables.

Variations: Crush a small clove of garlic into the meat mixture while it heats through.

Shepherd's Pie
Make as for cottage pie but use cooked meat from a roast joint of lamb (lean only). Add extra seasoning with ¼ teaspoon rosemary, ground to powder in a pestle and mortar, and 1 clove garlic, crushed.

Chicken Pie
Make as for cottage pie but use leftover chicken from a roast. Add extra flavour with finely grated rind of ¼ lemon and 1 heaped teaspoon finely chopped parsley.

TVP Pie
A very inexpensive, vegetarian dish. Make as for cottage pie but instead of meat use 1 slightly heaped tablespoon TVP mince, unflavoured.

Soak in the water for 10 minutes. Sprinkle in the flour and soy sauce with ¼ teaspoon mixed herbs (dried) or 1 level teaspoon fresh, finely chopped. Cook the mixture for 3 or 4 minutes before putting it into the pie-dish.

Fish Pie
Make as for cottage pie but instead of meat use poached white fish fillet—cod, haddock, whiting or plaice flakes. For flavouring use ¼ finely grated lemon. Instead of gravy make a cupful of white sauce

(see p. 85) and omit the soy sauce. A teaspoon of finely chopped parsley with 1 heaped tablespoon finely chopped prawns completes the base. Garnish with a sprig of parsley.

SAVOURY CAKES

You probably know these by several other names—rissoles, burgers, croquettes or even cutlets. Generally they have a poor reputation as all manner of cooked leftovers and dubious ingredients can be used to make them, while outwardly they all look innocently the same. The food industry loves them, especially junk food manufacturers, as they are cheap and easy to produce and market.

Considering the way they are constructed, it is easy to see how these rogues of the dinner plate and fodder for on-the-hoof eaters can step up in class to a much better food when fresh and imaginative top quality ingredients are used. Whether rissoles, burgers or whatever, the ingredients for good savoury cakes are as follows:

Base—soft breadcrumbs or mashed vegetable(s), especially potato.
Protein—raw or cooked meat, canned or fresh fish, TVP, cheese, nuts or egg, also combinations of these.
Flavouring—herbs, tomato purée, soy sauce, garlic, lemon juice, onion, spices, tomato ketchup, horseradish sauce.
Binder—egg, grated apple, tomato.
Coating—plain flour or beaten egg and fresh soft breadcrumbs.
Oil for shallow frying—sunflower or extra virgin olive oil.

NOTE: Savoury cakes can be baked in the oven as opposed to frying, in which case a coating may not be required and considerably less fat is used.

New attitude is required that allows food such as fresh fillet steak or salmon, best cuts of pork, lamb and beef, game and shellfish to be used for savoury cakes without feeling these ingredients are too classy for such a humble food. Just because certain people cannot chew, it doesn't follow they must be denied quality ingredients and variety for the rest of their days. In some cases it can mean upgrading the savoury cake to gourmet status—luxury soft options!

Presentation
For some strange reason, like some kinds of scampi and ham, commercial savoury cakes are to be found encased in strange coatings which have been dyed brilliant yellow or orange. Although these

137

are meant to represent breadcrumbs, I have yet to come across the gaudy-coloured breads that can be used to make crumbs such as these. Needless to say, the homemade variety is of a more gentle hue and looks perfectly appetising in normal bread colours.

Shapes
The traditional round, flat shape is easily achieved by hand-shaping, but then so are oblong, sausage and heart shapes. With a knife, square, rectangular, triangular and finger shapes are possible, too. Even bolder are fish, drumstick and fan shapes. Try a *coeur de la crème* mould for a perfect heart shape.

Making Savoury Cakes (1 serving)
Method: The cakes described on the following pages are all made in basically the same simple way. Ingredients are put into a bowl and mixed, then formed by hand into flattish cakes. They are cooked after just dusting with flour, and/or dipping in beaten egg and soft breadcrumbs. Shallow oil is used to fry them, with the cakes being turned once. Two or three minutes each side should be enough for pre-cooked ingredients but for raw kinds allow up to 10 minutes per side on a gentle heat. Avoid overfrying as this will make the food crisp.

Fish/Meat—use at least 3oz (80g) of the fish or meat per portion to make 2 savoury cakes.
Bread—one slice of bread made into crumbs in a coffee grinder or about 2 heaped tablespoons.
Potato—medium potato, boiled and mashed, will make a one-portion base. When you mash it add a small knob of soft margarine and a dash of milk. A hand potato masher is perfect for the job.
Beaten egg—break an egg into a saucer. Beat with a fork to mix the white with the yolk.

Savoury Cakes

Cod (Serve with tomato sauce)

1 portion baked or poached cod, mashed	1 heaped teaspoon finely chopped parsley
2 heaped tablespoons mashed potato	salt and finely ground pepper to taste

Tuna (serve with tomato sauce)

½ medium can tuna, drained and mashed

2 heaped tablespoons mashed potato

1 tablespoon tomato ketchup

salt and finely ground pepper to taste

1 heaped teaspoon finely chopped parsley

Sardine (serve with tomato sauce)

2 canned sardines, drained and mashed

1 tablespoon soft breadcrumbs

1 squeeze fresh lemon juice

1 heaped teaspoon finely chopped parsley or coriander

1½ heaped tablespoons mashed potato

finely ground pepper to taste

Chicken (serve with gravy)

1 portion lean cooked chicken meat, chopped very finely (no skin) or put through a mincer twice

1 heaped teaspoon finely chopped fresh parsley or mixed herbs

squeeze of lemon juice

¼ teaspoon soy sauce

2 heaped tablespoons mashed potato

salt and finely ground black pepper to taste

small pinch ground cloves

Beef (serve with gravy)

1 portion lean, cooked roast beef, put through a mincer twice

½ teaspoon made mustard or horseradish sauce

½ teaspoon soy sauce

salt and finely ground black pepper to taste

1 level teaspoon finely chopped parsley

2 heaped tablespoons mashed potato

Lamb (serve with gravy)

1 portion lean cooked roast lamb (leg is ideal), trimmed and put through a mincer twice

½ teaspoon dried rosemary, pounded with a pestle and mortar to a powder

¼ clove garlic, crushed

½ teaspoon soy sauce

salt and finely ground pepper to taste

2 heaped tablespoons mashed potato

139

Pork (serve with gravy)

1 portion cooked roast pork, trimmed and put through a mincer twice

1 tablespoon apple sauce, or very finely grated fresh apple

½ teaspoon soy sauce

¼ teaspoon dried sage, or ½ teaspoon fresh, finely chopped

2 heaped tablespoons mashed potato

salt and finely ground pepper to taste

TVP (vegetarian) (serve with suitable gravy)

½ oz natural flavour TVP mince, ground to powder in a coffee grinder and soaked in 1 tablespoon boiling water for 10 minutes

¼ medium onion, finely chopped and fried in 2 teaspoons sunflower oil

2 good pinches dried mixed herbs, or ½ teaspoon fresh, finely chopped

1 canned tomato, pips removed, finely chopped

1 tablespoon soy sauce

salt and finely ground pepper to taste

¼ teaspoon tomato purée

Bean, Nut and Cheese (vegetarian) (serve with suitable gravy)

2 heaped tablespoons mashed potato

1 heaped tablespoon baked beans, puréed

2 heaped teaspoons chopped nuts, pounded to powder with a pestle and mortar and put through a fine sieve

1 heaped teaspoon finely grated parmesan cheese

beaten egg to bind

salt and finely ground black pepper

Nut (vegetarian) (serve with suitable gravy)

white of two spring onions, very finely chopped

1 heaped tablespoon soft breadcrumbs

1½ teaspoons soy sauce

1 level teaspoon tomato purée

½ beaten egg

1 canned tomato, seeds removed, finely chopped

1½oz (40g) finely ground almonds

3 good pinches mixed herbs or ½ teaspoon fresh, finely chopped

finely ground pepper to taste

Cheese (vegetarian) (serve with tomato gravy)

white of 2 spring onions, very
finely chopped
2 heaped tablespoons mashed
potato
1½oz (40g) finely grated tasty
cheddar cheese (vegetarian)

milk to bind
1 canned tomato, pips removed,
finely chopped
1 heaped teaspoon finely
chopped fresh parsley

Ham and Cheese

Make as for cheese, but use 1oz (25g) cheese and 1 slice thin ham,
fat cut off, very finely chopped. Add half a beaten egg to bind. Use
the remaining beaten egg for egg and breadcrumbs.

white of 1 spring onion, very
finely chopped
1 teaspoon finely chopped parsley
2 heaped tablespoons mashed
potato
1 tablespoon finely grated tasty
cheddar cheese

1 thin slice lean ham, finely
chopped
½ teaspoon tomato purée
(optional)
¼ teaspoon made mustard
(optional)
½ beaten egg to bind

Savoury Cakes with Fresh Meat

The meat will need to be trimmed of all fat, gristle and bone and put
through a mincer twice. The onions should be chopped finely and fried
in 2 teaspoons sunflower oil before you make the savoury cakes.

Steak (serve with gravy)

1 small piece fillet steak about
2½oz (65g) put through a
mincer twice
¼ medium onion, finely chopped,
fried in 2 teaspoons sunflower
oil
2 small mushrooms, very finely
chopped

1 teaspoon soy sauce
2 heaped tablespoons fresh soft
breadcrumbs
salt and finely ground pepper to
taste
½ teaspoon made mustard

Lamb (serve with gravy)

3 medallions of lamb cut from 3
lamb chops, put through a
mincer, twice
¼ medium onion, finely chopped
and fried in 2 teaspoons sunflower oil

1 tablespoon redcurrant jelly
(jam)
salt and finely ground pepper
2 heaped tablespoons soft fresh
breadcrumbs
½ teaspoon soy sauce

Variations:

1 Instead of redcurrant jelly use ½ clove garlic, crushed and ½ teaspoon powdered rosemary (use a pestle and mortar and put through a fine sieve).
2 Omit redcurrant jelly. Serve with mint sauce.

Pork (serve with gravy)

lean from 1 pork chop, put through a mincer twice
¼ medium onion, finely chopped and fried in 2 teaspoons sunflower oil
1 tablespoon apple sauce

2 pinches dried mixed herbs or ½ teaspoon fresh, finely chopped
2 heaped tablespoons fresh soft breadcrumbs
½ teaspoon soy sauce
salt and finely ground pepper

NOTE: Pork must be properly cooked through.

Serving Suggestions for Savoury Cakes
The raw meat kind will require a good gravy and hot vegetables, puréed. The cooked meat and fish kind are best served with a suitable sauce. The vegetarian variety can be served with either a sauce or vegetarian gravy. See sauces and gravies, chapter 6. Suitable vegetables are puréed peas, carrots, broccoli, spinach and celeriac. Puréed cabbage can be served with the meat savoury cakes. As there is either potato or breadcrumbs in the savoury cakes, there should be no need to serve potatoes unless for a large appetite.

QUICK DINNERS

Quick Chicken Dinner
Make vegetable soup. Chop about 3–4oz (80–100g) lean cooked chicken until it is as fine as sawdust. Stir into soup. Add a little milk and stir in. Add more water if required. Taste. Adjust soy sauce and seasoning. Serve with 'dumplings' of mashed potato on top. Serve hot. See chapter 7 for vegetable soups.

Variation: Add 1 teaspoon finely chopped parsley or ¼ teaspoon thyme.

Quick Beef Dinner
Make vegetable soup. Chop slices of beef from a cold roast joint. Trim off fat and any gristle. Keep chopping until the meat is as fine as sawdust. Stir into soup. Add more water if required. Taste. Adjust

142

soy sauce and seasoning. Serve with 'dumplings' of mashed potato. Serve hot. See chapter 7 for vegetable soups.

*   *   *

Beef with Ginger (1 serving)

4oz (100g) rump steak
2 pinches salt
3 teaspoons sunflower oil
½ clove garlic put through a
  garlic press
small piece root ginger, about the
  size of a thimble, chopped
  very finely

1 tablespoon soy sauce
2 teaspoons dry sherry
1 spring onion, finely shredded
  and then finely chopped

Method: Sprinkle the steak with salt. Cut across the grain into wafer-thin slices. Cut across to make tiny squares. Heat the oil in a small frying-pan. Crush in the garlic and fry for a few seconds. Put in the tiny pieces of steak and ginger. Stir-fry for a minute. Put in the soy sauce and sherry. Stir and take off the heat. Sprinkle in the spring onions, stir and serve with stir-fry vegetables and boiled rice.

NOTES: If you find it easier, process the cooked steak in a mini-chopper with a little of the gravy. This recipe is unsuitable for anyone on an alcohol ban due to medication.

CURRY (2 servings)

This bears no resemblance to the real thing but is what most people would understand as curry. It comprises a rich gravy made with curry powder, meat or TVP and vegetables. It is served with rice, chutney and side dishes.

Chapatis represent a serious problem. They are extremely chewy and best avoided. The crisper varieties can be reduced to crumbs in a coffee grinder and sprinkled over the curry, but this will only produce the taste and not the texture.

Vegetarian Style Curry

½ medium onion, finely chopped
1 tablespoon sunflower oil
1 slightly heaped teaspoon mild
  curry powder
1 slightly heaped teaspoon finely

chopped coriander
¼pt (150ml) cold water
2 teaspoons tomato purée
2 teaspoons soy sauce
½ teaspoon sugar

143

1 level tablespoon sultanas, soaked in boiling water for 15 minutes, drained then finely chopped on a board

2 heaped tablespoons natural flavour TVP mince

8oz (225g) diced fresh vegetables in season—a mixture of carrots, swede, peppers, turnip, parsnip, celery, celeriac, green beans—whatever is available

1 small can tomatoes including liquid

1 slightly heaped teaspoon cornflour

to serve:

plain boiled rice

10 thin slices cucumber

½ banana

soft chutney

Method: Use a medium saucepan to fry the onion in the oil for 2 minutes while you stir. Add the curry powder and coriander. Stir-fry for another minute. Pour in the water and put in the prepared vegetables, tomato purée, soy sauce, sugar, prepared sultanas, TVP and tomatoes. Stir and bring to the boil. Turn down the heat and simmer with the lid on for about 20 minutes or until vegetables are tender. Stir in the cornflour mixed with a tablespoon of water. Heat and stir until the gravy has thickened. Put through a mouli into a bowl, using the cutter with the largest holes. Keep warm.

Chop the rice as small as you can. Put on to a warmed serving plate in a circle. Fill with curry. Finely chop the cucumber and serve separately on a saucer with the banana, mashed with a fork at the last minute. Chapatis, made into crumbs in a coffee grinder or very finely chopped, can be served in a bowl with a spoon.

Egg Curry

Make as for vegetarian curry but leave out the TVP. Serve instead with finely chopped hard-boiled egg on top of the curry, or, hard-boiled egg chopped and processed in a mini-chopper with 2 tablespoons of the curry. Allow 1 large egg per serving.

Beef and Vegetable Curry

Make as for vegetarian curry but leave out the TVP. After putting the curry through a mouli, return to the pan, adding 2 heaped tablespoons cooked finely minced beef. Cook for another 5 minutes while you stir. To make it more spicy, fry ¼ teaspoon finely chopped fresh ginger with a clove of garlic (put through a garlic crusher) in a tablespoon of sunflower oil. Add to the curry when you put in the meat.

CHAPTER 10

Puddings and Desserts

With a healthy diet including three pieces of fruit per day, puddings and desserts are a good way of using these up. There is no need to concentrate on milk merely because it will make soft puddings. Soft bread can be used in some puddings in slices or as crumbs.

Pastry is a problem as its very nature is crisp and chewy, but crumbles come into their own on top of fruit and comprise the same ingredients as pastry.

You will not find sorbets or ice-cream in this chapter. Problem mouths do not take kindly to a below-freezing assault, and the sugar content of sorbets, not to mention the level of fat and sugar in ice-creams, is usually excessive. See chapter 12 for a less healthy and more relaxed approach to puddings, but for everyday fare use this chapter.

Fresh Fruit Salad

Choose a juice as the base, e.g. orange, apple or pineapple. Select ripe fruit and prepare for the mini-chopper. All these are suitable: apple, pear, peach, nectarine, seedless grapes, banana (peeled), pineapple, strawberries, raspberries.

Have ready a tall sundae dish.

One by one process the fruit with a little of the base juice and sugar to taste. Add to the sundae dish in layers, finishing with a brightly coloured layer. Do not mix. Serve chilled from the fridge or at room temperature.

NOTE: You may find the banana is easier to mash with a little of the base juice rather than processing in the mini-chopper.

Stewed Fresh Fruit
Prepare fruit as indicated below, put into a saucepan and add enough water to prevent it going dry. Bring to the boil, then simmer until fruit is soft. Sweeten to taste with sugar or honey.

There are several fruits which stew well: apples, plums, apricots, peaches, pears, greengages, gooseberries, raspberries, blackberries, red- and blackcurrants, damsons and rhubarb. Apple is a good fruit to combine with plums, blackberries, red- and blackcurrants, raspberries and rhubarb.

Wash and pick over the fruit, which should be ripe. Cut out any bruised parts.

Plums, peaches, greengages, apricots. Cut the flesh away from the stones. Put through a sieve to remove skins after stewing until tender.
Damsons. Stew whole and remove stones when the fruit is soft.
Berries. Remove stalks and stew whole. Put through a sieve to remove pips when the fruit is soft enough. Only juice will be produced. Mix with stewed apple.
Rhubarb. Trim and cut into short lengths. Stew with the juice of an orange. Purée with a potato masher.

Stewed Frozen Fruit
Allow to defrost slowly then stew as for fresh fruit. A particularly useful product is fruits of the forest, a mixture of berries. This can be mixed with apple or used on its own to produce a magnificent rich juice, full of flavour. It needs sieving on account of the variety of pips it contains. (For the extra-sensitive mouth it may require straining through muslin too.) Frozen raspberries, blackberries and blackcurrants should be defrosted slowly and then stewed as for fresh. Always sieve to remove pips and skins.

Stewed Dried Fruit
Soak overnight in water to allow the fruit to swell. Put into a saucepan with enough water to cover. Bring to the boil and cook until fruit is tender. Allow to cool a little, chop, then put into a liquidiser. Blend to a thick purée.

Fruit Juice Blancmange—milk-free (2 servings)

For this dessert you will need stewed fresh fruit or canned fruit without its juice or syrup. Any of the following are suitable: peaches, pears, seedless grapes, stoned prunes, apricots, pineapple or raspberries.

2 portions stewed or canned fruit, liquidised and strained through a fine mesh sieve	sugar to taste water ¾oz (20g) cornflour

Method: Put the fruit juice into a liquidiser. Add enough water to bring it up to the ½pt (300ml) mark and sprinkle in the cornflour. Blend. Pour into a small saucepan and heat gently while you stir, until it has thickened. Sweeten to taste. Pour into two glass dishes or a wetted mould and leave to cool. When cold turn out on to a plate(s) and serve with teaspoons.

NOTE: A larger dessert can be made with two flavours, one on top of the other. The pear and grape versions can be improved by one or two drops of colouring (see p. 42).

Blancmange (2 or 3 servings)

This bears no resemblance to the packet type. It has much more flavour and brighter colours. Flavouring is made by blending fresh, canned or frozen (defrosted) fruit and water. Any fruit with skins and/or pips should be put through a fine mesh sieve.

¼ pt (150ml) strong fruit juice (see below) ¾oz (20g) cornflour (about 1 heaped tablespoon)	2 heaped tablespoons low-fat dried milk granules ¼ pt (150ml) water sugar to taste

Method: Mix the dried milk and water in a jug. Put 2 tablespoons of the fruit juice into a cup with the cornflour and mix to a smooth paste. Heat the milk, cornflour and fruit juice in a saucepan, stirring over a gentle heat. Bring to the boil and turn down the heat, continuing to stir for another 2 minutes. Add sugar to taste and stir well. Pour the thickened mixture into 2 or 3 glass dishes and leave to cool.

Suggested flavours:

- 4oz (100g) fresh or frozen raspberries
- small tin pineapple chunks or 2 fresh pineapple rings
- ½ medium tin apricot halves

- ½ medium tin peach halves
- 4oz (100g) blackcurrants (fresh or frozen)
- 4oz (100g) frozen fruits of the forest (without the strawberries)
- small can prunes, stoned.

Chocolate Dessert (serves 2)

2 tablespoons ground rice
½ pt (300ml) water
2 tablespoons low-fat dried milk granules
1 slightly heaped tablespoon drinking chocolate

few drops vanilla flavouring
1 slightly heaped tablespoon sugar
cooking chocolate to finish (optional)

Method: Put all ingredients into a small saucepan and stir well. Put over a gentle heat and bring to the boil, stirring. Cook for 2 more minutes, still stirring, until it is thick and smooth. Spoon into 2 glass dishes and allow to cool.

Grate about 3 squares of cooking chocolate into fine crumbs. Sprinkle over the desserts before serving.

Coffee and Walnut Dessert

Make as for chocolate dessert but omit drinking chocolate and instead of vanilla flavouring use 2 slightly heaped teaspoons instant coffee granules and 4 walnut halves, pounded in a pestle and mortar and sieved. Instead of the cooking chocolate, spoon over a little single cream or put on a blob of whipped cream.

Fruit Jelly (3–4 servings)

This is the only recipe in the book which contains gelatine (see chapter 2).

1pt (600ml) fruit juice (see below), sweetened to taste with caster sugar

½oz (15g) powdered gelatine

Method: Put about 4 tablespoons of cold fruit juice into a cup and sprinkle in the gelatine. Leave to soften for 5 minutes. Heat the remaining fruit juice almost to boiling point but do not let it boil. Stir the gelatine mixture and pour into the hot fruit juice. Stir until all the gelatine has dissolved. Pour into glass dishes and leave to grow cold and set. Serve cold from the fridge and eat within 12 hours.

Flavours: On no account use pineapple or kiwi fruit as they contain an enzyme which will not allow the gelatine to set. This still leaves

148

you with a good selection to choose from. Homemade jelly is far superior to the bought block jellies which comprise mainly sugar, artificial flavourings and colour. The homemade kind are made with fruit juice, no colourings and far less sugar.

Orange—freshly squeezed juice, from about 6 medium oranges and water.

Grape—use green seedless grapes, about 1lb (450g) blended with water in a liquidiser and strained through a fine mesh sieve.

Apricot—use a medium can of apricots with water. Blend to a liquid in a liquidiser.

Peach—as for apricot, using canned peaches or fresh, peeled and stoned.

Apple—use non-fizzy bottled apple juice.

Blackcurrant—stew 8oz (225g) fresh or frozen blackcurrants with water. Blend in a liquidiser. Put through a fine mesh sieve.

Fruits of the forest—stew 1lb (450g) frozen fruit with water. If strawberry pips are a problem remove the strawberries. Blend in a liquidiser and add water to make up to 1pt (600ml).

Stewed Apple (1 serving)
This need not be boring as flavours can be varied. If the apple is really good quality just leave it as it is; properly cooked it will taste superb.

1 medium Bramley cooking apple	small knob butter
2 tablespoons water	caster sugar to taste

Method: Peel and core the apple. Quarter and cut into thin slices. Put into the pan with the water and cook over a medium heat, stirring from time to time. After 5 or 6 minutes the apple will begin to purée of its own accord. Stir and cook until all the slices have disappeared. Take off the heat. Add the butter. Allow it to melt then beat to a smooth purée. Add the sugar to taste and beat again. Serve hot or cold.

Variations:
- Add the finely grated rind of ½ a small lemon.
- Add 3 pinches cinnamon or allspice.
- Serve with custard, single cream or unflavoured yoghurt.
- Soak one tablespoon of sultanas in boiling water for 15 minutes. Drain and chop as small as you can. Stir into the cooked apple with 3 pinches mixed spice or cinnamon.

- Finely chop 3 stoned dates. Cook with the apple.
- Use demerara sugar instead of caster.
- Add 1 heaped tablespoon frozen fruits of the forest (without the strawberries) when you cook the apple. When cooked, put through a fine sieve to remove pips. The colour will be a deep purple.
- Add a handful of blackberries before cooking the apple. When cooked, put through a fine sieve to remove the pips.

Baked Apples (2 servings)

2 medium-sized cooking   demerara sugar or runny honey
  apples   water

Preheat oven: Gas 4/180°C/350°F. *Position*: above centre shelf. *Baking time*: about 30 minutes.

Method: Cut out the cores of the apples and with the point of a sharp knife or an apple corer cut a line around the middle of each one (this gives the apples a chance to expand without bursting). Put the prepared apples into a shallow ovenproof dish and add about a cupful of water. Bake until the apples are soft. Remove the top skins. Spoon out the soft apple and put into individual bowls. Pour the juice over; sprinkle with sugar or drizzle with honey. Serve hot or cold, as it is or with a little single cream or hot with custard. (If convenient, serve the apple in the bottom skin.)

Variation: Sprinkle with 2 or 3 pinches of ground cloves or cinnamon or allspice.

Stuffed Baked Apples
Make as for Baked Apples but stuff the central cavity with one of the following:

- soft marzipan
- dried apricots which have been soaked, drained and chopped finely and a little finely grated lemon peel
- finely chopped fresh or canned mangoes
- sultanas which have been soaked, drained and finely chopped
- mixture of seedless raisins and sultanas which have been soaked, drained and finely chopped. Add 2 good pinches mixed spice, the finely grated rind of ¼ lemon, 2 teaspoons finely ground almonds and a teaspoon of melted butter. Mix well in a small basin.

Baked Bananas (1 serving)

Not much to look at but has a dazzling flavour and is simple to make.

2 small bananas (or 1 large)   sugar to taste
juice of 1 small orange

Preheat oven: Gas 3/170°C/325°F. *Position*: above centre shelf. *Baking time*: about 20 minutes.

Method: Grease a small ovenproof, shallow dish. Peel bananas, slice in half lengthways and lay in dish. Pour over the fruit juice and sprinkle with sugar. Bake and serve hot.

Baked Bananas with Passion Fruit

Method: Cut open a passion fruit. Spoon out the flesh and pips and press through a fine sieve. Only a small amount of purée will result but it will have a really strong flavour. Mix with the juice of 1 small orange. Make as for baked bananas above.

Scented Pears (2 servings)

Aromatic and delicate, a simple dessert that is light and fat-free. It does not have a particularly inspiring appearance but makes up for this with its lovely aroma.

2 Conference pears   caster sugar to taste
finely grated rind of ½ a lemon   water

Method: Peel, core and quarter the pears. Put into a small saucepan and sprinkle with the lemon rind. Add a little caster sugar and enough water to cover. Bring to the boil, then simmer until the pears are tender. Lift out the pears, chop then put in a mini-chopper with 2 tablespoons of the pan juices. Process to a purée. Divide between 2 bowls and spoon over 1 tablespoon of the juice. Allow to cool. Serve chilled from the fridge.

Lilac Pears (2 servings)

As delicately flavoured as its colour; this simple dessert will grace the best dinner table.

2 Conference pears   water
2 heaped tablespoons frozen sum-   caster sugar to taste
    merfruits (without straw-   ¼ level teaspoon cinnamon
    berries)

Method: Peel, core and quarter the pears. Put into a small saucepan with the summerfruits and enough water to cover. Sprinkle in a little sugar and the cinnamon. Bring to the boil and simmer until the pears are tender. Lift out the pears, chop and put into a mini-chopper. Strain the liquid from the pan through a fine mesh sieve. Put 2 tablespoonfuls into the mini-chopper with the pears and process to a purée. Taste and add more sugar if required. Divide between 2 bowls or glass dishes and spoon over a tablespoon more of the juice. Serve at room temperature with single cream or a dollop of unflavoured yoghurt. (For a very special occasion serve with a little whipped cream.)

Rice Fruit Dessert (2 servings)

This is a much more up-market sweet than rice pudding. It comes in a variety of interesting colours, depending on the fruit used.

2 portions stewing fruit (see suggestions below) sugar to taste	2 tablespoons ground rice water

Method: Cover the prepared fruit with water and bring to the boil. Simmer until tender. Allow to cool a little, then purée in a blender. Make up to ½pt (300ml) with water. Mix the ground rice in a cup with 2 tablespoons water until smooth. Put into a small saucepan with the puréed fruit. Mix well and heat gently while stirring for a few minutes until thickened. Add sugar to taste. Pour into individual dishes or into a small wetted mould. Leave to set. Serve cold.

Fruit with a strong flavour is best. Try the following suggestions:

Blackberries, raspberries or loganberries—4oz (100g) will be sufficient; put through a fine mesh sieve to remove pips.
Black- and redcurrants—4oz (100g) will be sufficient; put through a fine mesh to remove skins and pips.
Fruits of the forest—4oz (100g) will be sufficient: put through a fine mesh sieve to remove pips and skins.
Prunes—use half a medium-sized can or 10–12 prunes you have soaked and stewed yourself. Remove stones before blending and add a squeeze of lemon juice. You probably won't need any sugar.
Apricots—use 6–8 ripe fruit. Halve and remove stones before stewing.

Fruit Snow (2–3 servings)

It is difficult to imagine a simpler, softer, lighter dessert than this one. Use ripe, fresh fruit or else stewed, canned or cooked dried fruit. The secret is to strain the fruit to remove excess liquid and pips.

8oz (225g) approx. prepared   sugar to taste
fresh, canned, cooked dried or   2 egg whites
stewed fresh fruit

Method: Make a thick purée of the fruit of your choice using a liquidiser. Put through a sieve into a bowl. Add sugar to taste and stir well. Whisk the egg whites until stiff and forming peaks. Sprinkle in a teaspoon of sugar and whisk again. Use a metal spoon to fold into the fruit purée. Pile up into glass dishes and serve chilled from the fridge soon after making. Some suggestions for the fruit are:

Fresh ripe fruit—soft pears, peaches, nectarines or apricots, raspberries, strawberries, pineapple (you may need to add a little water to the liquidiser).
Canned fruit—pears, pineapple chunks, peaches, apricots, guavas, prunes.
Cooked dried fruit—prunes, apricots, peaches.
Fresh or frozen stewed fruit—apple, blackberry and apple, apple and summerfruits, apricots, greengages, plums, peaches with a few raspberries, apple and blackcurrants, gooseberries.

NOTE: Always remove all stones from cooked fruit before liquidising.

Eve's Pudding (3 servings)

Base: *Topping*:
3 cooking apples   2oz (50g) soft margarine
caster sugar to taste   3oz (80g) self-raising flour
¼ teaspoon cinnamon   1 large egg, beaten
water   2oz (50g) caster sugar
                                 milk to mix

Preheat oven: Gas 4/180°C/350°F. *Position*: centre shelf. *Baking time*: about 30 minutes.

Method: Peel and core the apples. Slice thinly into a greased pie dish and sprinkle with a little sugar, the cinnamon and 1 tablespoon water. Put the margarine, flour, egg and caster sugar into a mixing bowl. Mix and beat to a soft, creamy consistency, adding a little milk if you think it is too thick. Spread evenly over the apple base and bake. After 10 minutes cover the dish with greaseproof paper and continue baking (this is to prevent a tough crust). Serve warm from the oven with single cream or custard.

Pear and Chocolate Eve's Pudding
Make as for Eve's Pudding but omit cinnamon and use ripe Conference pears. Add 1 level tablespoon of cocoa to the topping, using 2½oz (65g) flour instead of 3oz (80g). Serve with single cream or custard.

Plum Eve's Pudding
Make as for Eve's Pudding but use 9 ripe eating plums such as Victorias. Cut out the stones and chop the fruit. If you think the skins will be a problem, peel the plums before stoning. Put them in a basin and pour boiling water over them. The skins will split and can be peeled off easily.

Greengage Eve's Pudding
Make as for plum Eve's Pudding but use 12 ripe greengages.

Blackberry and Apple Eve's Pudding
Stew a handful of blackberries in a little water until tender. Put through a wire mesh sieve. Add to the apple slices and continue as for Eve's Pudding. Omit cinnamon.

Peach Eve's Pudding
Make as for Eve's Pudding, but instead of the apple use 2 or 3 ripe peaches. Rub the skin all over with the flat of a knife and peel off. Remove stones and slice fruit thinly. Omit cinnamon.

Apricot Eve's Pudding
Make as for Eve's Pudding but use fresh, ripe apricots instead of apple. Take out the stones and slice as thinly as you can.

Fruit Crumble (2 servings)
Crumble topping has the same ingredients as pastry but does not reach the kneading and rolling-out stages. This keeps it soft. Eat hot or cold.

Base:
4 heaped tablespoons suitable part-stewed fruit (see suggestions below)
sugar to taste

Topping:
2 heaped tablespoons plain flour
1 slightly heaped tablespoon soft margarine
1 tablespoon sugar

Preheat oven: Gas 6/200°C/400°F. *Position*: top shelf. *Baking time*: about 12–15 minutes.

Method: Put the flour and margarine into a mixing bowl and rub in with the fingers until the mixture resembles breadcrumbs. Stir in the sugar. Put the part-stewed fruit into an ovenproof dish and sprinkle the topping over it in a thick layer. Bake and serve on its own, hot with custard, or, cold with single cream or unflavoured yoghurt.

Suggestions for the fruit base:

apple
blackberry and apple (sieved)
pear with a few pinches of
    cinnamon
bananas (just slice, don't stew)
apricots (stoned)
prunes (stoned) with finely grated
    rind of ¼ lemon

peaches (stoned)
apple and raspberry (sieved)
apple and summerfruits (sieved) .
greengages (stoned)
plums (stoned and sieved)
3 plums, 1 apple and 1 pear with
    a few pinches of allspice

Peel and stone the fruit as appropriate.

Stew the fruit in a little water until almost tender. Strain in a fine sieve and put into the dish (the fruit will finish cooking as the topping cooks). Avoid fruit from which the juice runs as this will make the crumble soggy. Gooseberries, raspberries and currants should not be used, for this reason.

Tinned fruit can be used if strained through a fine sieve.

Peaches, apricots, pears, prunes (stoned) should be chopped after straining and put into the dish. Pineapple needs processing in a mini-chopper as it is rather fibrous.

NOTE: Any juice left over from straining the fruit can be saved and used when serving.

Hot Fruit Meringue (2 servings)
This is a useful fat-free recipe as the fruit can be varied and individual portions can be made. Use ramekins (cocottes) which are ovenproof.

3oz (80g) stewed fruit for the
    base
sugar to taste

1 egg white
2oz (50g) caster sugar

Preheat oven: Gas 3/160°C/325°F. *Position*: above centre. *Baking time*: about 15 minutes, until meringue is golden and lightly set.

Method: Put the stewed fruit, sweetened to taste, into 2 greased ovenproof ramekins. Whisk the egg white in a small basin until stiff. Continue whisking and add a tablespoon of the sugar. Stop whisking and gently fold in the remaining sugar. Pile on top of the stewed fruit. Bake and serve hot.

Stewed fruit options for the base

- Cooking apple plus finely grated rind of ¼ lemon.
- Cooking apple and fruits of the forest, puréed.
- Cooking pears puréed and 3 pinches cinnamon or finely grated rind of ¼ lemon.
- Plums, stones removed, puréed, 3 pinches allspice.
- Damsons, stones removed.
- Greengages, stones removed.
- Blackberries and cooking apple, puréed and put through a fine mesh sieve to remove pips and skins.
- Apricots, stones removed, puréed.
- Mashed banana with juice of 1 passion fruit (put through a fine mesh sieve).
- Cooking apple and raspberries, puréed and put through a sieve to remove pips.

Fruit on Bread (1 serving)
Quick to prepare, this simple hot pudding can be made all year round.

2 teaspoons butter	1 portion stewed fruit—apple,
1 slice soft bread made into	peaches, stoned plums,
crumbs	apricots, stoned greengages
	sugar to taste

Method: Put the butter into a small frying-pan. Fry the crumbs, turning them over. Sprinkle with sugar and mix well. Turn on to a warm plate in a heap. Flatten and top with the fruit. Sprinkle with sugar and serve.

NOTE: The stewed fruit should be processed to a purée in a mini-chopper if necessary.

Bread and Butter Pudding (2 servings)

5 to 6 slices soft bread	1 egg
soft margarine	8fl oz (225ml) water
1½oz (40g) sultanas	2 level tablespoons low-fat dried
mixed spice	milk granules
sugar	

Preheat oven: Gas 5/190°C/375°F. *Position*: middle shelf. *Baking time*: about 35—40 minutes.

Method: Put the sultanas into a cup and cover with boiling water. Leave to swell for half an hour. Cut the crusts off the bread and discard. Spread slices with margarine. Cut into halves. Grease a shallow baking dish and cover the base with slices, margarine side down. Drain and chop the sultanas as small as you can. Sprinkle half into the dish with a little sugar and a few pinches of spice. Cover with another layer of slices, the remaining chopped sultanas, a little sugar and pinches of spice. Cover with the remaining slices, margarine side down and sprinkle with spice. Whisk the water and dried milk in a basin. Add the egg and whisk again. Pour over the bread through a fine mesh sieve. Leave for 30 minutes or so to allow the bread to absorb the egg and milk mixture. Bake, loosely covered with greaseproof paper. Serve hot from the oven, on warmed plates. Cut off any crisp pieces.

Soft Steamed Fruit Pudding (makes 4 servings)
For the filling use cooking apples, plums, gooseberries with apple, peaches, pears, apricots, greengages, or any mixture. The fruit should be ripe and prepared (peeled and stones removed as appropriate).

Special soft pastry	*Filling*
2oz (50g) soft margarine	8oz (225g) raw, prepared fruit
4oz (100g) ground rice	2 tablespoons sugar
3oz (80g) finely grated eating apple	1 tablespoon water

Method: Put the pastry ingredients into a bowl and blend with a fork. Knead with the fingers to make a stiff paste, using a little more ground rice if it feels too sticky. Liberally grease a 1pt (600ml) pudding basin with soft margarine. Take two thirds of the pastry and roll into a ball. Flatten and place in the bottom of the basin. Using your fingers, press the pastry round and up the sides of the basin so that it is lined as evenly as possible and extends to just ½in (1cm) below the rim of the basin. Make the remaining third of the pastry into a round, flat lid by pressing it out with the fingers.

Cut the fruit into thin slices and put half into the lined basin. Sprinkle with 1 tablespoon of the sugar. Put in the rest of the fruit slices and the remaining sugar. Pour over the tablespoon of water, or more if the fruit is dryish, and put on the pastry lid using a spatula. Press the edges on to the lining all round the edge to seal in the fruit. Steam (see pp. 41–2). When it is ready, lift out the pudding by the string handle. Remove string and greaseproof. Put a warmed serving plate over the top of the basin. Hold the plate and basin firmly together and turn upside down. Avoid shaking it but leave for a few seconds and the pudding will drop on to the plate. Carefully lift off the basin and serve in wedges with custard.

NOTE: This recipe is intended to replace steamed suet pudding which has a tougher pastry.

Steamed Sponge Pudding (2–3 servings)
The lightest of sponges, cooked gently on the hob. Flavour it, top it, serve with custard or a sauce for variety. See pp. 41–2 for advice on steaming.

2oz (50g) soft margarine	3oz (80g) self-raising flour
2oz (50g) caster sugar	flavouring—see Cup Cakes,
1 egg	p. 161; use the same flavours

Method: Put the margarine and sugar into a large bowl. Mix to a cream. Whisk the egg in a cup. Beat into the bowl and sieve in the flour. Fold in gently, then mix to a soft dropping consistency with the flavouring of your choice. Add a little water if it turns out too stiff. Grease a suitable pudding basin and spoon in the mixture. It should come not more than two thirds up the basin as it needs room to rise. Cover and steam for about 1–1¼ hours. Turn upside-down on to a plate and serve hot with custard or sauce.

For topped versions, put 2 tablespoons of one of the following into the basin before you put in the uncooked sponge mixture:

jelly jam—any flavour	any soft stewed fruit (sieved if
jelly marmalade	necessary)
golden syrup	any finely chopped canned fruit
	(drained first).

Serve all of these with custard.

Baked Egg Custard (2 servings)

9fl oz (265ml) water	1 egg, beaten
2 really heaped tablespoons low-fat dried milk granules	½oz (15g) caster sugar
	nutmeg

Preheat oven: Gas 2/160°C/300°F. *Position*: above centre shelf.
Baking time: about 45 minutes to 1 hour.

Method: Boil water in the kettle and measure into a jug. Leave for a minute and stir in the milk granules. Put the egg and sugar in a basin. Add the hot milk while you whisk. Have ready a greased pie dish. Strain the mixture into the dish, through a fine mesh sieve. Grate a little nutmeg on top and stand the dish in a roasting tin containing cold water. Bake and serve from the dish. Good with a little single cream and a sprinkle of sugar, or just the sugar.

NOTE: Slow baking is essential for a smooth-textured custard.

Queen of Puddings (2 servings)
A dark-coloured jam or fruit looks best between the pale yellow base and the white meringue. A very stylish pudding.

6fl oz (175ml) milk	1oz (25g) fine white breadcrumbs
2 strips of lemon rind (about ⅓ lemon)	1 large egg, separated
1 tablespoon butter	1 generous tablespoon jelly jam or puréed stewed fruit
2oz (50g) caster sugar	

Preheat oven: Gas 4/180°C/350°F. *Position*: above centre shelf. *Baking time*: 15 to 20 minutes for base plus 8–10 minutes for topping.

Method: Put the milk into a small pan and add the strips of lemon rind. Heat very gently, then turn out the heat and leave to infuse for 10 minutes. Discard the rind. Begin to heat gently again and put in the butter and 3 teaspoons of the sugar. Stir until the butter has melted. Add the breadcrumbs and egg yolk. Mix well. Spoon into a small, well greased, ovenproof pie dish. Wait 10 minutes then bake until set. Take out of the oven and leave to cool a little. Spread with the jam. Whisk the egg white until stiff. Whisk in 2 teaspoons of the sugar. Whisk again. Fold in the remaining sugar using a metal spoon. Spoon over the baked pudding. Finish baking at Gas 2/160°C/300°F and serve warm on warmed tea plates.

NOTE: Do not over-bake the meringue or it will go crisp.

CHAPTER 11

Cakes and Teatime Food

Tea used to be what people ate when most of us had our main meal at midday. Nowadays the main meal tends to be in the evening, so few people eat 'tea' as a meal. This is a pity as it is an easy meal to assemble without a great deal of washing-up.

A full tea would be soft bread and butter with jam as optional, little soft sandwiches and soft cake. (See chapter 13 for a range of suitable sandwiches.) Just cake on its own is a more likely event, regarded really as a sweet snack, falling somewhere between a food and an entertaining treat. Struggling with dried fruit or a tough sponge made from a bought sponge mix is no fun, although the average person would not imagine these to be a problem for the non-chewer. However, they are indeed a problem and need to be sorted out for comfort and enjoyment of teatime food.

CUP CAKES

These are useful little buns, but for non-chewers need to be baked avoiding a tough crust on top. There are two ways of coping with this problem. Either shape the buns before baking so that they produce a flat top that can be sliced off, or, cover individual buns with flattened cake papers so that a soft top will result. Many flavours can be enjoyed and they can be left plain or iced for variety.

CAKES AND TEATIME FOOD

Cake Mixture (makes 6)

2oz (50g) soft margarine
2oz (50g) caster sugar
2½oz (65g) self-raising flour

1 egg
flavouring (see list below)
milk to mix

Preheat oven: Gas 5/190°C/375°F. *Position*: above centre shelf. *Baking time*: 12–15 minutes.

Method: Put all ingredients into a mixing bowl and mix/beat to a creamy consistency, adding a little milk if it is too stiff. Have ready a patty tin lined with 6 cake papers. Using 2 teaspoons, three-quarters fill the papers. Bake. Take out of the oven and cool on a wire rack.

Suggested flavours for cakes and buns

Orange—finely grated rind of ½ orange.
Lemon—finely grated rind of ¼ lemon.
Vanilla—5–6 drops vanilla flavouring.
Ginger—½ teaspoon dried ginger.
Chocolate—1 heaped teaspoon cocoa and 3 drops vanilla flavouring.
Spice—1 level teaspoon mixed spice.
Cinnamon—½ level teaspoon cinnamon.
Coffee—1 slightly heaped teaspoon instant coffee granules dissolved in 1 teaspoon hot water.
Almond—1 heaped teaspoon finely ground almonds and 3 or 4 drops almond flavouring.
Passion fruit—put the contents of 1 fruit (halved) through fine mesh sieve to remove pips.
Caraway—soak 1 teaspoon caraway seeds in 1 tablespoon boiling water. Strain and use the resulting liquid. (On no account use the seeds in the buns.)
Sultana—soak 1 heaped tablespoon sultanas in boiling water for 30 minutes. Strain and chop fruit finely on a board.
Currants—as for sultanas and add ¼ teaspoon finely grated lemon rind.
Seedless raisins—as for sultanas.

Finishings for buns to make Cup Cakes (see p. 166 for icing)

Orange, lemon and vanilla buns—top with plain white water icing.
Ginger—use white water icing with a little grated lemon rind mixed in.
Chocolate—use white water icing and add 1 slightly heaped teaspoon sieved cocoa or drinking chocolate. While still not set, sprinkle with finely grated cooking chocolate. (optional)

Coffee—dissolve 1 teaspoon instant coffee granules in a teaspoon of hot water. Make a water icing with it plus a little more water.

Coffee and walnut—make as for coffee but add 2 teaspoons powdered walnuts (paste). Put through a fine mesh sieve before it starts to set to remove any pieces of nut that are not fine enough.

Pink vanilla—use a few drops beetroot juice or fruits of the forest juice to colour white water icing. Use on vanilla buns.

Chocolate and apricot—spread the tops of buns with apricot jelly jam and cover with chocolate water icing (see chocolate).

Miniature soft gateaux—make the vanilla or plain cake mixture but only fill the cake papers half full. Put a tablespoon of puréed drained canned fruit on top and bake. Cool on a wire rack and top with a blob of whipped cream. Peaches, apricots and pears are all suitable. The fruit will sink into the cakes to make a soft top.

Madeira Cake

The traditional topping of sugar and citron peel is not used for this plain cake. Serve for tea or in fingers with fruit salad.

4oz (100g) caster sugar	8oz (225g) self-raising flour
4oz (100g) soft margarine	milk to mix
2 eggs	finely grated rind of ½ lemon

Preheat oven: Gas 4/180°C/350°F. *Position*: centre shelf. *Baking time*: 1¼ hours.

Method: In a mixing bowl, cream the sugar and margarine until light and soft. Beat the eggs in a basin. Add alternately to the margarine mixture with the flour, beating in well after each addition. Add a little milk to make a soft consistency and stir in the lemon rind. Have ready a greased 7in (18cm) round cake tin, lined with greased greaseproof paper. Put in the cake mixture. Use a knife to make a slight well in the centre and bake. After 15 minutes cover with greaseproof paper to stop a hard crust forming. Once baked, leave in the tin for a minute before turning out on to a wire rack to cool, removing the papers.

If the top is not soft enough, cut if off before serving each piece.

Orange Cake
Make as for Madeira Cake but substitute the finely grated rind of 1 orange for the lemon rind.

Rich Madeira Cake
Make as for Madeira Cake but use butter instead of margarine.

Gingerbread

This cake keeps well and grows moister after 2 or 3 days.

7oz (200g) self-raising flour
2 level teaspoons powdered
  ginger
5oz (130g) soft margarine
6oz (160g) black treacle

4oz (100g) soft brown sugar
1 tablespoon water
2 eggs
1 teaspoon finely grated lemon
  rind

Preheat oven: Gas 3/170°C/325°F. *Position*: centre shelf. *Baking time*: 1 to 1¼ hours.

Method: Sift the flour into a large bowl with the ginger. Mix well. Put the margarine, treacle, sugar and water into a saucepan. Stir over a gentle heat until the margarine has melted. Put into the flour bowl. Mix/beat well. Add the eggs and lemon rind and beat again. Have ready a greased and lined 7in (18cm) diameter cake tin. Put in the mixture and bake. Press your finger on the cake. If it leaves no impression it is cooked. Leave to cool in the tin for about half an hour, then turn out carefully on to a wire rack to grow cold. Store in an airtight container.

Gugelhopf

A remarkably light, semi-sweet fruit cake. The fruit and rinds can be varied. Choose from apricots, raisins, sultanas, pitted prunes or peaches and orange or lemon rind. It is baked in a special mould with a central funnel. This recipe is for a 6in (15cm) diameter tin, available from kitchen shops.

sunflower oil for greasing
2oz (50g) suitably prepared dried
  fruit (see p. 39 for advice)
2oz (50g) soft margarine
¼oz (7g) instant/Easyblend yeast
6oz (160g) plain wholemeal flour
  (fine grade)

5 tablespoons warm milk
2oz (50g) caster sugar
1 egg, beaten
rind of 1 orange, finely grated
juice of 1 orange

Preheat oven: Gas 5/190°C/375°F. *Position*: above centre shelf. *Baking time*: about 35 minutes.

Method: Soak the dried fruit in boiling water for an hour. Drain in a sieve. Chop on a bread board as finely as possible. Gently melt the margarine and leave to cool a little. Use a pastry brush to paint the inside of the tin with oil, including the funnel. (It is important to make sure all the surface is covered).

Put the yeast and flour into a large bowl and mix well. Add the milk, margarine, sugar, egg, orange juice, rind and chopped fruit. Mix, then beat to a soft consistency. Turn into the mould and leave to rise in a warm place until the dough reaches the top of the tin. Bake then turn out of the tin and cool on a wire rack. Eat freshly baked for tea or a snack. Can also be used as a pudding with custard.

Light Sponge Cake
A really hot oven is required to bake this cake.

3 large eggs	*Finishing*:
4oz (100g) caster sugar	jelly jam
3oz (80g) self-raising flour	icing sugar
1oz (25g) melted soft margarine	
1 tablespoon hot water	

Preheat oven: Gas 7/220°C/425°F. *Position*: top shelf. *Baking time*: 10–12 minutes.

Method: Whisk the eggs and sugar in a basin until thick. Sieve the flour twice into a basin to keep it light. Fold in gently to the egg/sugar mixture using a metal spoon. Stir in hot water. Have ready two 7in (18cm) round sponge tins, greased with the melted margarine and base-lined with greased, greaseproof paper. Divide the sponge mix equally between them, spreading them evenly with a knife. Bake. (Press gently but firmly in the centre. If they spring back they are cooked.) Leave for a minute then turn out on to a wire rack to cool. Peel off the lining paper. Sandwich with jelly jam and dredge the top with icing sugar.

Precautions for soft options
No matter how light your sponge, it will have a thin crust on top which needs to be removed. There are several ways of tackling the problem. One is to use greaseproof paper which can be peeled off, taking the crust with it. Any remaining crust can be cut off thinly with a sharp knife, or it can be lightly scored in a criss-cross pattern and scraped off.

To remove the 'crust' from the bottom of the sponge, wait one minute after turning out of the tin, then peel off the greaseproof. Cut all round the sides with a sharp knife as neatly as you can. Score the top lightly to make little squares and carefully scrape off the layer of brown squares, back to the white sponge.

Victoria Sponge

Eaten freshly made this is a soft plain cake.

4oz (100g) soft margarine
4oz (100g) caster sugar
2 eggs, whisked

4oz (100g) self-raising flour
jelly jam and icing sugar to
finish

Preheat oven: Gas 5/190°C/375°F. *Position*: just above centre shelf.
Baking time: 20 minutes.

Method: Put the margarine and caster sugar into a bowl. Mix/beat until light and soft. Gradually beat in the egg. (If it starts to curdle add a little of the flour.) Sprinkle in the flour through a sieve and fold in gently (don't beat) with a metal spoon. Have ready 2 greased and floured 6in (15cm) sponge tins. Divide the mixture between the two tins and bake. Test by pressing a finger. If no impression remains the sponges are cooked. Turn out of the tins on to a wire rack. When cold, cut off the edges with a bread knife and take off top crust as for Light Sponge. Sandwich together with jelly jam. Sprinkle top with icing sugar.

Variations: Replace 1 tablespoon of the flour with 1 tablespoon cocoa for Chocolate Sponge.

NOTE: The bases of the tins can be lined with greased, greaseproof paper, ensuring a perfect turnout.

Orange Teabread

½oz (15g) instant/Easyblend
    yeast
8oz (225g) plain flour
2oz (50g) soft margarine
½ teaspoon salt
1 generous tablespoon golden
    syrup
1oz (25g) brown sugar

3oz (80g) rolled oats, ground to
    a flour
grated rind 1 orange
¾pt (450ml) boiling water
juice of 1 orange
cold water
melted margarine for brushing

Preheat oven: Gas 7/220°C/425°F. *Position*: above centre shelf.
Baking time: about 45 minutes.

Method: Blend the flour and yeast in a bowl. In a second (large) bowl mix the margarine, salt, syrup, brown sugar, oat flour and orange rind. Pour in the boiling water. Make the orange juice up to ¼pt (150ml) with cold water and add to the oat flour mixture. Stir well then begin to add the flour gradually. Mix to a soft dough. Knead until it feels smooth. Put into a greased bowl and brush with melted margarine. Cover with food film and put in a warm place to rise. When doubled in size turn out on to a floured worktop and knead for a minute. Shape to fit a 2lb (1kg) greased loaf tin. Leave to rise again, uncovered. When doubled in size, bake, turning down the heat after 15 minutes to Gas 4/180°C/350°F. Turn out of tin and cool on a wire rack. Serve sliced and buttered with crusts cut off.

NOTE: The oats can be quickly ground into a flour using a coffee grinder.

Water Icing
Sieve icing sugar into a small basin. Stir in a few drops of hot water and mix with a spoon to a thick liquid. Use a knife to spread over cakes and leave to set. (Three heaped tablespoons of icing sugar will ice 12 cup cakes or a sponge.)

CHAPTER 12

Treats and Celebration Food

This over-the-top chapter is included to balance the moderation of the rest of this book. The food in this category bears little relation to health but is important on a psychological level. Everyone needs to celebrate from time to time—not every day, please note! The idea of a treat is that it is something rare, to be enjoyed, not something eaten frequently just because it is delicious. We all tend to reach for the double cream as the ultimate enricher of food for a special occasion, as well as too much sugar, chocolate and egg yolk, but such fare is purely entertainment food and lacks the underlying health message found in all the other chapters. It is rather rich, not easily digested and should be served in small portions.

Asparagus Soup (2 servings)

7oz (200g) pack of medium-sized asparagus spears
¼ medium onion, peeled and chopped finely
1 tablespoon sunflower oil

½pt (300ml) water
2–3 teaspoons soy sauce
salt and fine ground pepper
2 tablespoons single cream

Method: Wash the asparagus spears thoroughly. At the bottom of each one, cut off and discard about 1in (2.5cm). Cut off the tips and put to one side. Slice remaining stems into short lengths—these will form the basis of the soup. Gently fry the onion in the oil for 3–4 minutes while you stir (avoid browning as this spoils the colour of the soup). Pour in the water and put in the pieces of stem. Bring to the boil and add 2 teaspoons of soy sauce. Simmer for about 7 or 8 minutes, then add the tips. Bring back to the boil and simmer for another 4 minutes or until all the asparagus is tender. Allow to cool for a few minutes, then liquidise in a blender. Taste and add more soy sauce if required, as well as seasoning. Reheat gently without letting it boil. Pour into 2 warmed soup plates and swirl a tablespoon of cream into the middle of each one.

Spaghettini al Salmone (serves 1)
A rather special starter with smoked salmon and cream.

2oz (50g) smoked salmon (strips will do)	2oz (50g) vermicelli made into tiny noodles (see p. 64), or homemade tiny pasta squares
2 tablespoons single cream	finely ground black pepper

Method: Cut the smoked salmon into tiny squares. Put into a small basin with the cream and leave to marinate for about 1½ to 2 hours, covered. Cook the pasta for 3 minutes in a pan of boiling water. Drain in a fine mesh sieve. Put the salmon and cream mixture into a heavy-based saucepan and heat very gently (on no account let it boil). Pour over the hot pasta, season with fine pepper and stir. Serve immediately.

Luxury Savoury Cakes (for special occasions)
See p. 138 for instructions under 'Making Savoury Cakes'.

Salmon and Asparagus (serves 1)

1 small portion fresh salmon (fillet), poached in white wine and water, mashed with a fork	1 tablespoon single cream
	2 heaped tablespoons potato, mashed with butter
1 heaped teaspoon finely chopped fresh parsley	salt and finely ground pepper to taste
8 small asparagus tips, poached in water until tender, drained and mashed	

NOTE: Remove any skin from the salmon and check it for bones. Egg and brown breadcrumbs will be the best finish for this luxury version of savoury cakes.

168

TREATS AND CELEBRATION FOOD

Pheasant (serve with gravy, 1 serving)

1 portion cold pheasant (breast), very finely chopped	1 heaped tablespoon mashed potato
1 tablespoon bread sauce with powdered cloves	2 heaped teaspoons soft bread-crumbs
1 tablespoon redcurrant jelly (jam)	¼ teaspoon soy sauce
	salt and finely ground pepper to taste

NOTE: Pheasant is apt to be rather dry. Add a teaspoon or two of gravy to the mix if it seems so.

Grouse (serve with gravy)
Make as for pheasant, but use breast of grouse.

Party Chipolatas
Make the Skinless Pork Sausages from p. 78 but shape into small chipolatas. Fry for less time and serve with cocktail sticks. Ideal for a party.

Cooked Soft Meringue
Use for topping desserts instead of ice-cream.

2 egg whites	1 tablespoon water
5oz (130g) caster sugar	1 drop vanilla essence

Method: Whisk the egg whites until stiff. Put to one side while you make the syrup. Using a small pan, dissolve the sugar in the water. Add the vanilla essence, then boil rapidly to make a thick, clear syrup. Pour gradually on to the egg whites while you whisk. Stop when the mixture is shiny and smooth and will hold its shape. Cool and use within the hour.

Fruit Alaska (4–6 servings)
A very pretty dessert that can be varied. Use one fruit, or two different ones, and cooked meringue topping. Serve in sundae glasses to show off the colours.

Lemon

2oz (50g) cornflour	2 egg yolks
½pt (300ml) water	2oz (50g) caster sugar
1oz (25g) butter	cooked soft meringue (see above)
finely grated rind and juices of 2 small lemons	

Method: Use a small saucepan to blend a little of the water with the cornflour. Put in the rest of the water with the butter. While you stir, bring to the boil, slowly. Continue cooking for another 2 or 3 minutes and add the lemon rind and juice. Lastly stir in the egg yolks and sugar. Stir and cook for another ½ minute. Pour into sundae glasses and leave to cool. Serve chilled with a generous topping of cooked meringue.

Variations: Instead of the lemons use:
Orange—oranges. You will need two.
Lime—fresh limes. You may need three.
Apricot—4 or 5 fresh apricots or a medium can of halves drained with the finely grated peel of 1 small lemon. Blend the fruit and top up with water to make ½pt (300ml).
Peach—use 2 fresh peaches or 1 medium can of peach slices, drained. Blend the fruit and top up with water to make ½pt (300ml).
Pineapple—4 slices fresh pineapple or 1 medium can chunks, liquidised with the juice. Top up to ½pt (300ml) with water.
Raspberry—8oz (225g) fresh or frozen raspberries. Blend the fruit with a little water. Put through a fine sieve to remove pips. Make up to ½pt (300ml) with more water. You may need more sugar if they are sour.
Strawberry—if there is a problem with the pips, trim as suggested on p. 40. Allow 12oz (350g) large fresh berries. If the pips are not a problem use 8oz (225g). Blend and make up to ½pt (300ml) with water.
Fruits of the forest—use 8oz (225g) frozen fruits of the forest. Stir in a little water, blend and put through a fine strainer. All pips except strawberries will be removed. If strawberry pips are a problem use a mixture without strawberries.

Two-flavour Fruit Alaska
If making a dessert with two different fruits, make two half recipes. Put alternate spoonfuls into the glass dishes so that they are not all mixed together as one flavour. Top with the cooked meringue. A selection of good combinations:

- peach and raspberry
- pineapple and strawberry
- lemon and lime
- orange and lemon
- apricot and raspberry.

Strawberry Fool (5–6 servings)

An extravagant and rich dessert. If the strawberry pips might be a problem, use 1½lbs (700g) strawberries and trim as described on p. 40.

1lb (450g) strawberries
6oz (160g) caster sugar
½pt (300g) double cream

Method: Wash and hull the strawberries. Put into a saucepan and mash to a pulp with a potato masher. Stir in 1oz (25g) of the caster sugar. Put the cream into a bowl. Whisk until thick and soft. Gradually add the rest of the sugar, whisking in each addition. Stop when the cream will stand in peaks but is still soft. Fold the purée into the cream without mixing them too much. Serve in glass dishes and chill in the fridge.

NOTE: Be careful not to overbeat the cream or it will separate.

Raspberry Fool

Make as for strawberry fool, using fresh raspberries. Put through a fine mesh sieve to remove the pips.

Chocolate Mousse (2–3 servings)

1½oz (40g) plain cooking chocolate
2 small eggs, separated
1 tablespoon sherry

2 tablespoons whipped cream
grated chocolate to decorate

Method: Place a basin over a pan of hot water. Put in the chocolate, broken into pieces. Stir until it has melted completely, then add the egg yolks and sherry. Mix well. Whisk the egg whites until they will almost form peaks. Fold into the chocolate mixture, carefully, using a metal spoon. Divide between 2 or 3 ramekins and put into the fridge to set. Serve decorated with a blob of cream and sprinkle with grated chocolate.

NOTE: A very rich dessert. Do not serve to anyone who is on an alcohol ban due to medication.

Sponge Gâteau (8–10 slices)

Make a Victoria Sponge or a Light Sponge Cake, (see chapter 11). Remove the top crust by scoring the top with a sharp knife, just cutting through the crust to make small squares. Scrape off carefully with a knife to the sponge underneath. Trim crust away from the edges.

Process a drained tin of peaches or apricots in a mini-chopper (or chop finely by hand). Spread one layer of the sponge with half the fruit purée and the other with whipped cream, sweetened slightly with icing sugar and flavoured with vanilla flavouring. Sandwich together. Cover the top with more whipped cream. Decorate with teaspoons of the fruit purée in a regular pattern. Sprinkle in between with toasted almond flakes, powdered in a coffee grinder. Serve within an hour of making.

If preferred, spread cream around the sides and sprinkle with powdered toasted almond.

Soft Celebration Cake (makes 12–16 slices)
A special cake for birthdays, Christmas, weddings and christenings. Traditional cakes of this kind are designed to be eaten as a rare treat. They are heavy, chewy, solid with dried fruit and covered with rock-hard icing over almond paste. The tough skins on the vine fruits are the major problem. If minced finely before baking they produce a bread pudding-like texture which is just as chewy. If mashed with a fork after the cake is baked the fruit does not respond and remains stubbornly chewy. The citrus peel used in dried fruit mixes also defies chewing but it can be replaced by finely grated rind and so is not such a problem. The non-chewy redeeming features of traditional cake are spices, black treacle, ground almonds, eggs, sugar and margarine which provide the basic structure of the cake's flavour.

There is no aroma like that of a rich fruit cake baking slowly in the oven. With this new recipe you will be able to enjoy this without the worry of how to eat the cake afterwards. Soft almond paste is used for covering the top and thin water icing for the finishing.

It is not a cake for keeping, unless you want to freeze it. The texture is too light and soft for a tall cake so it is made in sponge tins and sandwiched together. It is just as enjoyable for those who can chew as those who cannot, so can be passed round with confidence. (Do not be surprised at requests for 'seconds'.)

Cake:

8oz (225g) specially prepared dried fruit mixture (see p. 39)
5oz (130g) fine grade self-raising wholewheat flour
½ teaspoon cinnamon
½ teaspoon mixed spice
4 good pinches nutmeg
2 large eggs
4oz (100g) soft margarine
2 generous teaspoons black treacle
4oz (100g) soft brown sugar

2oz (50g) ground almonds
5–6 drops almond flavouring
2 tablespoons sherry or brandy (optional)
finely grated rind of ½ lemon
finely grated rind of ½ orange

Finishing:
sherry or grape juice (non-fizzy)
apricot jelly jam
soft marzipan (see p. 174)
icing sugar for rolling out
2oz (50g) icing sugar for topping
hot water

Preheat oven: Gas 5/190°C/375°F. *Position*: above centre shelf.
Baking time: about 25 minutes.

Method: Put the dried fruit into a basin and cover with boiling water. Leave for an hour to plump up, then strain in a sieve and chop finely on a board, sprinkling with a little of the flour to keep the pieces separate. Mix the remaining flour in a basin with the spices. Beat the eggs in a basin using a fork. Put the margarine, black treacle and sugar into a large mixing bowl and mix to a cream. Beat in the egg mixture alternately with the flour and spices mixture. Stir in the ground almonds, almond flavouring, alcohol (if using) and rinds. Add the prepared dried fruit. Mix again.

Have ready two 7in (18cm) diameter sponge tins, greased and lined with greased greaseproof paper. Turn the mixture into the 2 tins, spreading with a knife to put more around the edges than in the centre, ensuring a flat top to the cakes. Bake for 10 minutes then cover each one with a sheet of greaseproof to stop the tops becoming too baked. Continue for the remaining baking time. Take out of the oven and put on to a wire rack. Leave for 2 minutes to shrink from the sides of the tins. Turn out on to the wire rack and leave until cold, still with the paper on.

Finishing the cake
Peel off the top papers. Prick the top of each cake all over with a fork. Drizzle each one with 2 or 3 teaspoons of sherry*. Allow it to soak in for a few minutes and soften the cake. Peel off remaining papers. Have ready the soft marzipan. Spread the bottom of one

* Some people will be on an alcohol ban due to medication. Use grape or apple juice (non-fizzy) instead of sherry if this is a problem.

cake with jelly jam. Put the other cake on top and press together. Spread the top sparingly with jelly jam, to hold on the almond paste. Press out the paste with your fingers to fit, on a piece of greaseproof paper, using icing sugar. Place upside-down on the top of the cake, and peel off the paper. Trim and mend as required. Leave uncovered to dry a little for 2 or 3 hours. (Do not leave too long or it will harden.

Sift the 2oz (50g) icing sugar into a basin. Add very little hot water and mix into a thick, shiny icing. Spread over the almond paste using a spreading knife dipped in hot water. Leave to set. Dress with decorations (see p.199) and a cake frill appropriate to the festivity. (On no account use pins to secure these.) Place on a cake board or a plate with a paper doily. Serve on tea plates with cake forks or even spoons. Eat within 2 or 3 days. Keep covered with food film or in an airtight container.

For a more showy cake, also cover the sides with soft almond paste and icing. Pipe water icing decoration around the bottom edge and on the top.

NOTE: This kind of cake, is designed as a celebration food. People who are ill or frail will not thrive on such food, but there is a great psychological advantage in having a special cake that suits everyone for a particular celebration.

Soft Marzipan

Bought marzipan usually goes rock hard. This marzipan will stay soft. Use for celebration cakes and for soft-centred chocolates. See pp.172, 176 and above.

2oz (50g) finely ground almonds	1oz (25g) caster sugar
1oz (25g) icing sugar	3 drops almond flavouring
egg yolk to mix	1 teaspoon water

Method: Mix all ingredients together, adding enough egg yolk to bind it. Knead really well to a wet, sticky paste. Wrap in a double layer of food film and store in the fridge. Use within 3 or 4 days. It will defy rolling out with a rolling-pin. Make flattish pieces and press out by hand. Press edges together to 'mend' it.

TRIFLES

Trifles have rather a poor reputation, as leftovers can be used to make them and they tend to be a little 'samey'. The classic tipsy trifle contains crunchy macaroons and is sprinkled with flaked almonds, so it needs a departure from this for a soft options version.

Sherry Fruit Trifle (1 serving)
Use a vanilla cup cake (without icing)—see p. 160. Cut in half and sandwich back together with jelly jam. Chop into small pieces and put into the bottom of a glass trifle dish. Spoon over 2 or 3 teaspoons sherry. Finely chop 5 drained canned peach slices and use to spread over the sponge. Cover with 3 tablespoons vanilla custard. When cool, cover the top with whipped cream. Finely chop another 2 or 3 peach slices and use to decorate the top.

Variation: Instead of peach slices use canned apricot halves. They can be quite sour so taste one and sprinkle with sugar if necessary.

NOTE: This recipe is unsuitable for anyone on an alcohol ban due to medication.

Black Forest Trifle
Cut a small wedge of chocolate sponge (p. 165) or a cup cake (p. 160) without icing. Cut in half and sandwich with jelly jam. Put into the bottom of a glass trifle dish. Have ready half a portion of stewed summerfruits (without the strawberries) puréed in a mini-chopper. Sweeten to taste and put through a fine mesh sieve. Spoon over the sponge. Cover with 3 tablespoons chocolate blancmange and leave to set. When cold cover the top with whipped cream and sprinkle with grated cooking chocolate in the centre. A mint leaf at a jaunty angle will set if off nicely.

Party Trifle
Make a larger version of either Sherry Fruit Trifle or Black Forest Trifle in a large glass dish. Serve on tea plates.

CHOCOLATES

The problem with bought chocolates is their size and hard fillings. Attempts to cut them up result in shattering of the chocolate coating; also it rather takes away the pleasure to half-destroy them even before they are eaten. Even the soft-centred types need to be bitten into and chewed. Another problem is the decorations—whole nuts, chopped nuts, crystallised flowers or an extra application of hard chocolate.

Miniature chocolates with soft centres would seem to be the answer. Unfortunately they don't exist in a commercial form so will have to be made at home. This may sound difficult, but in fact they are quite easy to make. A variety of soft centres is possible and they will dissolve in the mouth. Either soft marzipan or royal icing is used as a base, flavoured with fruit juices, peppermint, liqueurs or coffee. You will need a miniature kind of skewer for dipping the centres into the chocolate: a large darning needle is ideal.

Cooking chocolate can be bought at supermarkets from a section displaying baking ingredients. Milk, plain or white are available. They are best melted in a double boiler—i.e. a small basin set over a larger one containing hot water. Break the chocolate into squares before putting in the top pan. Keep the water in the lower pan hot and the chocolate will melt and stay runny.

The most useful base for the centres is royal icing which only needs a small amount of flavouring and will stay soft.

Royal Icing for Centres

½ egg white
1 teaspoon fresh lemon juice
4oz (100g) icing sugar, sifted

few drops flavouring—see suggestions below

Method: Beat the egg white lightly in a basin. Add the lemon juice and sift in the icing sugar. Beat until smooth. (Softness does not indicate that more icing sugar is required but rather more beating.) It should be stiff enough to stand up in peaks. Add the flavouring of your choice, by the drop, and beat again. Use a teaspoon to take a small amount and press it flat, on a plate dusted with icing sugar. Cut into tiny squares or diamonds.

Flavourings: Strong or concentrated fruit juice—raspberry, passion fruit, fruits of the forest, blackcurrant, lemon or lime juice, peppermint or other bought flavourings; liqueurs such as Tia Maria, Curaçao, Grand Marnier, apricot brandy, cherry brandy, etc; instant coffee granules dissolved in a minute amount of hot water.

Fruit flavours are made by mashing a few ripe berries or fruit flesh through a fine mesh sieve. Lemon requires a few drops of fresh juice, likewise lime. Some fruit can be used raw (raspberry, passion fruit) and just rubbed through a sieve. Others need to be stewed in a little water to get the juice out. Many flavourings are available from supermarkets (do not confuse them with colourings).

If you are making a selection of centres, and not just one, make peppermint after you have finished any others. Its flavour gets everywhere as it is extremely strong.

Soft marzipan can be used in the same way as royal icing (see p. 174). No extra flavouring is required.

Finishing: Melt squares of cooking chocolate in a double pan. Have ready the tiny flavoured centres and a sheet of baking parchment (non-stick). Spear each centre with a darning needle, dip in the chocolate, all over, and put on to the baking parchment to set and harden. Put into a glass dish to serve.

NOTE: Although it all sounds ridiculously fiddly, the results can be excellent and will undoubtedly bring a great deal of pleasure to chocolate lovers who have had to give them up. Soft options chocolates are designed to just melt in the mouth.

Chocolates flavoured with liqueurs are unsuitable for anyone on an alcohol ban due to medication.

EXTRA-SPECIAL SANDWICHES*

Smoked Salmon
A thin slice of smoked salmon as large as your hand will make two sandwiches. Use a sharp knife to cut into thin strips, then cut across to make tiny squares. Spread soft brown bread sparingly with butter. Cut off the crusts. Cover one half of the bread with the salmon, spreading it over with a knife, as evenly as possible. Squeeze a few drops of lemon juice over it and put on the tops. Cut into tiny triangles. Garnish with a lemon twist and either a parsley sprig or watercress.

Smoked Salmon, Cream Cheese and Chives
Make as for smoked salmon, adding a layer of cream cheese and a sprinkle of finely chopped chives. The top piece of bread can be left unbuttered.

Lobster
Make as for prawn (see p. 187) using tender pieces of lobster, fresh lemon juice and good mayonnaise.

* See chapter 13 for instructions.

CHAPTER 13

Packed Meals, Picnics, Sandwiches and Snacks

A regular lunch box means you will need a supply of plastic bags, plastic boxes and containers, screwtop jars, food film, vacuum flasks and some kind of container to hold them all—a large plastic box, basket or cool box can be used depending on what food is required. In summer keep food cool in a cool box with special freezer packs. Cool boxes are rather bulky because they are insulated but are extremely effective. The freezer packs are kept in the freezer until required. As soon as you return home, put them back in the freezer for the next time.

A soft options picnic or packed meal is quite different from an ordinary one. Think of it as special.

The vacuum flasks can be used for hot soup, hot water for tea or coffee, or cold drinks and milk shakes. Take a supply of dried milk to go in tea or coffee as well as tea bags and instant coffee.

Try to balance a packed meal with solid food and liquid, a high-protein food (egg, fish, meat, milk, cheese), high-carbohydrate food (bread, potatoes), fruit (as juice, stewed or fresh fruit) and an extra such as yoghurt, a few soft options chocolates (see p. 175) or a piece of soft cake or a bun (see chapter 11).

See p. 130 for soft meat slices. Hard-boiled eggs can be mashed and put in a small container. Small cans of salmon, tuna and sardines can be packed with a tin-opener if they don't have a ring-pull. Put salad dressings in small screwtop jars (mustard jars are ideal). Pack fruit juice in a plastic beaker with a snap-on lid or a screwtop bottle. Yoghurt travels well in a small jar. You will find all kinds of soft sandwiches later in this chapter and yoghurts in chapter 5 with juices and milkshakes. Some of the desserts in chapter 10 are good travellers and many of the soups in chapter 7 will be welcome on a cold day.

It is possible to buy wide-necked vacuum flasks which will take a hot meal—large chemists and pharmacists usually stock them. Avoid greens as part of the meal as they do not respond well to being left warm. Hot puréed beans and mashed potato (for baked bean fans) makes a friendly meal.

Most soft options salads will not survive, but peeled, de-seeded and chopped tomatoes will. Cooked puréed beetroot, cold boiled and mashed potatoes and finely chopped white of spring onion can be used for salad. Put the spring onion in a screw of food film and sprinkle it over the potato and beetroot just before eating.

Cheese such as cheddar and cheshire can be finely grated and wrapped in greaseproof paper before putting into a plastic bag. Cottage cheese probably needs mashing. Pack back into the original container and cover the top with food film.

The sandwiches that follow are ideal for packed meals and picnics but the bread *must* be kept moist to stop it drying out. Putting it in a box is not enough. Wrap in lettuce leaves and put into a sealed plastic bag, or put the sandwiches into food film, put them into a container, cover with two layers of kitchen paper lightly wrung out in cold water and put on the lid. The sandwiches will stay delightfully moist. Make sure the food film completely wraps them.

Keep your packed food and drinks containers all in one place in the kitchen so that you don't have to keep looking for them. Always wash the containers, dry and put them away to avoid them lying about, getting in the way and being lost.

Keep a special set of cutlery or even buy plastic cutlery at the supermarket which can be discarded after use. Put in spare kitchen paper, a table napkin or paper napkins when you make a packed meal. Mugs for liquid and plates will complete your equipment. China is heavy and apt to get broken. Kitchen shops and department stores have good plastic mugs, plates and so on. Avoid hideously garish colours. White or cream may seem dull but you'll never get fed up with them and food always looks good with these quiet colours.

SANDWICHES

Experience has shown me that there are cooks who really cannot make a sandwich. This is sad because they can be a marvellous finger food and one with which it is easy to feed someone. In one nursing home I visited the sandwiches were made early in the morning for the inmates' tea, nine or ten hours later. By the time they were served they were dry, curled up and leathery. They were inedible for any patients who *could* chew, let alone those who couldn't.

The sandwiches I saw in hospital were made from the worst quality, cheap, plant-baked bread. Although intended for people who couldn't chew, they were large and still had the crusts on. Not surprisingly they were all wasted and the patients left unfed and hungry. Let me now put this sorry tale aside and address the issue properly.

Normally sandwiches would be on the banned list for soft options food, as by nature they can require a considerable amount of chewing. However, with the appropriate bread, a soft purée filling, and crusts cut off, they can be a valuable and tasty addition to the non-chew diet.

Points to bear in mind

1 Bread needs to be fresh, soft and enjoyable.
2 Unless the sandwiches are to be eaten immediately they need special wrapping to keep them soft and moist.
3 Special soft fillings need to be made—a wide variety is possible.
4 To prevent the soft filling squeezing out during making they need a different approach from ordinary sandwiches.
5 Attractive presentation is important to stimulate appetite and make the sandwiches look special.
6 Sandwiches need to be very small so that they can be put straight into the mouth.

Your aim should be to produce a mini melt-in-the-mouth type of sandwich that only needs to be moved around the mouth with the tongue and sucked before swallowing. (Call on your feelings of empathy. Imagine that you yourself cannot bite or chew. How would you fare on your sandwiches? When you have made some, put one in your mouth. Deliberately avoid chewing and see how you get on.)

Suitable equipment

Use a large cutting board as making sandwiches can create a lot of crumbs and mess. Have ready your serving plate or storage container, kitchen paper and food film if required. A shaped butter knife is ideal for spreading fillings as well as butter or margarine. Although it is tempting to use the bread knife for spreading it is best used for just cutting the bread.

Suitable ingredients

All the bread recipes in chapter 4 are suitable for soft options sandwiches. If you are relying on shop-bought bread use a freshly baked loaf and choose one you know will have a soft texture (this could be difficult). Some sliced breads are cut thickly for toast and will not be suitable. Other loaves will be days old, already drying out and tough. In the end you may actually find it more convenient to bake your own bread, which puts you in control of the situation rather than leaving you at the mercy of the supermarket.

Although it seems wasteful to cut off the crusts, they need not be wasted and they will make excellent breadcrumbs. Grind in an electric coffee grinder. Store in a clean plastic bag and use up quickly. If you are planning on keeping crusts to make crumbs, cut them off the bread slices before you spread on the butter or margarine.

Making soft options sandwiches

With soft fillings there is a problem. As the knife presses down to cut through the sandwich the filling squeezes out. Obviously a different approach is required to ensure the filling stays between the bread slices. To make a soft options sandwich, cut two slices of soft bread. Cut off the crusts, making sure one slice is slightly smaller than the other. Spread both slices with soft margarine or butter. This will help hold the bread together if it starts to go into crumbs. Cover the largest slice with a soft filling—see the list of suggestions that follows. Cut the remaining smaller slice into small neat squares. Place these on top of the filling as neatly as you can, butter side down. Now cut down between the squares, through the filling and the bottom slice of bread, using the space between the squares as a guide. By using this method there is only pressure on the bottom slice of bread and the filling stays put. As it is rather fiddly to make, finish cutting it actually on the serving plate; this will save moving the little sandwiches about after they are made.

Making soft fillings

For soft sandwich fillings the mini-chopper comes into its own, provided you understand its limitations. Ideally you should be aiming at soft paste that will spread easily. If too moist and soft, the filling will squeeze out between the slices of bread. Too dry and it will confound the mini-chopper and be too coarse. The knack is to get it just right—soft, spreadable and tasty. Here is a selection of sandwich fillings and toppings which can all be made easily.

Banana

Put a small peeled banana on a saucer, chop with a knife then mash with a fork, adding a little soft brown sugar. Mash until you have a smooth, shiny purée. The filling will gradually turn brown but the taste will not be affected at all.

Banana and Cream

Make as for banana, but instead of buttering the bread when you make the sandwich, spread with double cream, preferably whipped.

Egg

Boil an egg (preferably free range and organic) for 8 minutes. Plunge into a basin of cold water and leave to cool for a few minutes. Peel off the shell and rinse under the cold tap. Chop coarsely and put into the mini-chopper with a tablespoon of suitable mayonnaise, salt and pepper to taste. Process to a smooth paste.

Curried Egg
Make as for egg, adding a few pinches of mild curry powder (do not make it too hot). Season to taste. An extremely tasty filling with a pungent aroma!

Egg and Cress
Make as for egg but add ½ packet washed and chopped cress.

Egg and Tomato
Prepare a tomato as described on p. 40. Chop the flesh and put into the mini-chopper with a chopped hard-boiled egg, seasoning to taste and a good pinch of caster sugar. Process to a purée.

Egg and Watercress
Make as for egg adding a handful of watercress leaves, coarsely chopped.

Ham and Egg
Make as for egg, adding ½ slice lean chopped ham and ⅛ teaspoon made mustard (optional).

Egg and Parsley
Make as for egg, but add 1 tablespoon chopped parsley.

Asparagus
Simmer asparagus tips in water for about 8–10 minutes until tender. Strain and cool. Put into the mini-chopper with 1 tablespoon suitable mayonnaise. Process to a green purée. Season to taste. Use soft brown bread spread with butter.

Tomato
Prepare as described on p. 40. Finely chop the flesh on a board and season to taste with salt, pepper and a pinch of caster sugar.

Watercress
Use the washed leaves from about ¼ bunch/packet watercress. Chop coarsely by hand then put into the mini-chopper with ½ tablespoon suitable mayonnaise. Process and sandwich between slices of soft brown bread spread with soft margarine.

SOFT OPTIONS

Cheese

Cream cheese, cottage cheese, marscapone and finely grated cheddar or cheshire are the most suitable cheeses for sandwiches. There are cheese spreads available but they are usually highly processed. Beware soft cheeses with added flavours like nuts and fruit. Of the soft cheeses, brie, camembert and cambozola might be acceptable if just the centre is used. However, even these are inclined to be a little rubbery and tough.

Cheese and Date

Mash 1 heaped tablespoon cottage cheese with 1 teaspoon single cream. Stone 2 or 3 Deglet Nour dessert dates. Chop as finely as you can. Mix into the cheese and use generously as a filling. Be sparing with the soft margarine when you butter the bread.

Cheese and Chives

Wash 8 chives. Snip as finely as you can with kitchen scissors and put into a cup with 1 heaped tablespoon cream cheese. Stir in a teaspoon or two of milk if the cheese is too stiff. Mix well and spread between plain soft bread—no need to butter the bread.

Cream Cheese

Best spread on unbuttered soft bread, preferably brown. Mix with a little milk if it is too stiff.

Cheese and Pickle

Use a soft pickle or chutney (see chapter 14) or one that you can process in the mini-chopper. Remove any pieces which escape the blades so that you are left with just a purée. Two teaspoons per round of soft bread should be ample. Spread the bread with soft margarine and sprinkle the bottom slices with very finely grated cheddar or cheshire cheese. Spread the top slices with the puréed pickle or chutney and press together.

Cheese and Tomato

Lightly spread the soft bread with soft margarine. Cover the bottom slices with a generous layer of very finely grated cheddar or cheshire cheese. Cover with peeled and de-seeded, finely chopped tomato and press on the top slices of soft bread.

For cream cheese and tomato omit the margarine. Spread cream cheese on top and bottom slices of soft bread so that the tomato is arranged between them, or mix together before spreading.

PACKED MEALS, PICNICS, SANDWICHES AND SNACKS

Cheese and Beetroot

Finely grate cooked beetroot (not easy and rather messy). Mix with mashed cottage cheese to make a brilliant pink filling. Use between buttered slices of soft bread.

Salmon

Drain a small can of red salmon. Turn out on to a saucer and mash with a fork. Take care to mash the bones as well as the fish. Add a tablespoon of suitable mayonnaise and mash again to a smooth paste. Use between unbuttered slices of soft brown bread. Press firmly together.

Salmon and Shrimp

Mash 1 heaped tablespoon drained, canned salmon or fresh poached. Put into the mini-chopper with a tablespoon of mayonnaise. Wash a heaped tablespoon of peeled shrimps under the cold tap, using a wire sieve. Chop first on a board and add to the mini-chopper with a few drops of fresh lemon juice. Use with soft brown bread.

Sardine

Best sardines to use are skinless and boneless. Drain the oil out of the can and put the sardines on a plate. Mash with a fork, adding a tablespoon of mayonnaise. Use between unbuttered slices of soft brown bread. Press together firmly.

Sardine and Tomato

Make as for sardine but substitute tomato ketchup for the mayonnaise.

Salmon and Cucumber

Drain a small can of red salmon or use a little cold fresh salmon. Put into the mini-chopper with a tablespoon of suitable mayonnaise and 8 thin slices of cucumber, chopped. Process to a soft paste and season to taste. This is an extra-moist filling due to the cucumber. Use with soft brown bread.

Tuna and Mayonnaise

Drain canned tuna and flake the fish into the mini-chopper, using about half the can. Add 1 slightly heaped tablespoon suitable mayonnaise and process until soft and smooth. Use with unbuttered soft bread.

Tuna and Salad
Use ¼ can drained tuna. Put into the mini-chopper with a few watercress leaves or ¼ packet cress, chopped. Add ½ peeled and de-seeded tomato and 1 tablespoon suitable mayonnaise. Process to a wet paste. Drain for a few minutes in a small wire sieve to take off excess liquid. This filling may be more suitable for an open sandwich, spread thickly and garnished with a sprinkle of finely chopped parsley.

Chicken
As meat and poultry are essentially fibrous in structure, chopping is not enough to make a soft filling. Use a few tender pieces of cooked chicken such as meat from the breast. Put it through the mincer. This should produce a sticky filling which can be improved with a tablespoon of suitable mayonnaise, 2 or 3 drops (only) of soy sauce and seasoning to taste. Go easy on the soy sauce which is best mixed into the mayonnaise and then added to the minced chicken. If any soft stuffing is available, use instead of mayonnaise.

Beef
Treat this in the same way as chicken, adding a little made mustard or horseradish sauce with the mayonnaise. Cut off and discard any fat.

Soft Meat Slice Sandwiches
See p. 130 for soft meat slices. The slices must be set and cold before they can be used for sandwiches. Cut soft bread slices, remove crusts and spread the bread with soft margarine. Cut meat slices to fit the bread and sandwich between two layers. If using chutney, mustard, etc., spread (or dot) on the top layer of bread before pressing it on firmly. Use a sharp knife to cut the sandwich into small squares.

If using chutney you will need special soft chutney—see chapter 14. Other spreads to use are redcurrant jelly, apple jelly, horseradish sauce and made mustard. (Tomato ketchup or brown fruit sauce (bought table sauces) can also be used if preferred.) Try the following combinations:

- dabs of mustard with ham or beef soft slices;
- spreading of soft chutney with chicken, turkey, ham, beef or pork soft slices;
- light spreading of horseradish sauce and beef soft slices;
- other fillings to consider are homemade or bought soft patês (not coarse).

Beef Dripping and Juices

This is definitely a nostalgic sandwich filling. Spread soft bread sparingly with the soft fat made by straining off fat and juices from a roast joint of beef and allowing them to cool. Underneath the fat the rich brown juices from the beef will have formed a kind of sauce. Spread this over the dripping and season with salt and pepper.

Cheese and Walnut

Use a soft cream cheese. Chop 3 or 4 walnut halves and put into a coffee grinder. Grind, remove any stubborn pieces and discard. Put the finer pieces into a mortar and pound with a pestle until they form a paste. Mix with the cream cheese, adding a little milk if too stiff. (People who cannot chew often long for some familiar taste associated with a chewy food, but if the nuts are not reduced to a paste they will be painful in the mouth.)

Prawn

Although prawns look soft they are quite chewy. Put 2 tablespoons of peeled prawns into a sieve. Rinse thoroughly under the cold tap. Shake and pat dry with kitchen paper. Chop first on a board, then put into the mini-chopper with 1 tablespoon suitable mayonnaise and a few drops of lemon juice. Process, season and use between soft brown bread spread with soft margarine.

Crab

Make as for prawn, using both colours of crabmeat or tinned crab.

Nostalgia, tastes remembered and cravings are all important and should be considered when catering for other people. (I shall never forget the old lady in a nursing home who was served pilchard sandwiches. Enraged, she threw them out of the open window, plate and all. 'What do you think I am—a cat?' she shrieked!)

The following three fish fillings come firmly under the heading 'tasty'. They also have a strong smell. However, this is what some people like about them. On the other hand, it is what makes some people hate them.

Bloater

A little goes a long way, so buy the smallest can available. Mash one heaped tablespoon to a paste, using a fork. Add a tablespoon of soft breadcrumbs that have been soaked for a few minutes in water and drained in a sieve. Avoid using any of the bones.

SOFT OPTIONS

Pilchards
Make as for sardines.

Kipper
A nightmare filling to make due to the bones. Use part of a cooked fillet and mash with a little melted butter. Pick out any little bones that you can see. If you think the taste is too strong, mash in soft breadcrumbs soaked in a little water and drained. Season with pepper to taste, but not salt.

See also p. 177 for Extra Special Sandwiches—Smoked Salmon, Smoked Salmon, Cream Cheese and Chives, and Lobster.

Open Sandwiches
These have only a bottom layer of soft bread (with the crusts cut off), spread with soft margarine or butter. The topping can be quite generous. Putting the bread on the serving plate before spreading on the topping makes it easier to manage. By using more than one topping per sandwich they can be quite adventurous, colourful and stylish. A bold garnish will set off any sandwich well and lift it out of the ordinary. Use edible garnishes of finely chopped parsley or watercress, puréed, peeled and de-seeded tomato, mashed hard-boiled egg. These can be put on the actual sandwich. Decorations such as tomato flowers, parsley, watercress and celery leaves should be put on the serving plate rather than on the actual open sandwich.

Some people will prefer a small knife and fork to cut up the sandwich themselves. Other people will need it cut into small squares before serving. Once again, this is easier to accomplish on the serving plate to avoid moving the squares about.

SLICES

There is something very comforting about the simplicity of a slice of bread spread with a tasty topping. Bread and jam is hopefully part of everyone's childhood. Here are a few nostalgic slices than can still be enjoyed, albeit in a new way.

Jam
See chapter 14 for information on suitable jam. Cut slices of soft bread. Cut off the crusts. Butter or spread with soft margarine. Spread with suitable jam and cut into small squares on the serving plate.

188

Marmalade
See chapter 14 for information on suitable marmalade. Make as for jam.

Honey
The best honey for a slice is the thick type, runny honey being stickier and apt to run off. Butter soft brown bread and spread with honey but not right to the edges. Cut off the crusts. Cut into small squares on the serving plate. As these are bound to be sticky, a damp cloth may be needed as well as a napkin.

Honey and Cream
Cut the crusts off soft bread and spread with honey. Top with a layer of whipped cream. Cut into small squares on the serving plate.

Treacle
Cut the crusts off soft bread. Spread with butter or margarine. Drizzle with golden syrup off a spoon. A sticky delight which will need the attention of a damp cloth for the hands after eating.

Yeast Extract
Cut thin slices of soft bread. Spread with soft margarine and then little dabs of yeast extract. Spread them a little as the flavour is very strong.

Garlic and Olive Oil
Cut slices of soft white bread. Slice a clove of garlic in half. Use half to rub over the bread. Drizzle with a good-tasting extra virgin olive oil. Cut off the crusts. Not quite the same as croustades but still a good taste for people who miss them.

Other Spreads
See sandwich fillings for banana, banana and cream and many other fillings which can be used as spreads for slices. See also p. 195.

Chip Butties
Although most people's experience of these will be as a joke, they do have serious addicts, particularly those who enjoyed them as children. There are many regional variations but basically they comprise a sandwich with a filling of hot chips and a table sauce. Cut 2 slices of soft bread and cut off the crusts. Take freshly fried hot chips and wrap in greaseproof. Keep warm for about 5 minutes or

longer until they have lost their crispness and are soft. Cut each one in half lengthways and place on one piece of bread, covering it completely. Spread ketchup or sauce over the chips after seasoning with salt to taste and press on the top piece of bread. (As the chips will have been fried in oil there is no need to butter the bread.) Cut into small squares and serve while the chips are still warm, on a warmed plate.

NOTE: Use homemade chips made with soft, floury varieties of potato—King Edwards or Cara—fried in sunflower oil or ovenbaked (see p. 119). Don't let them become too crisp by frying too long.

SNACKS

All kinds of food will serve as a snack. The soft sandwiches in the previous few pages and the simple slices are probably the first type of snack that springs to mind. Others are a slice of soft cake or a soft bun, a small pizza or a bowl of soup with either small squares of soft bread, soft breadcrumbs or miniature dumplings. A dish of yoghurt, a mashed jacket potato with cheese or puréed baked beans, or a piece of fruit pie will be welcome as a between-meal filler. Chapter 5 and chapters 7–11 all have possible snacks for people with good appetites.

Bumble

This is for fans of baked beans and fried bread or toast. Purée a portion of baked beans with its sauce in a mini-chopper. Make 1 generous slice of soft bread into crumbs. Melt a tablespoon soft margarine or butter in a frying-pan. Fry the crumbs lightly, turning them over. Heat the puréed baked beans in a small saucepan. Sprinkle half the fried crumbs on to a warmed plate. Spoon over the bean purée and top with the remaining crumbs.

CHAPTER 14

Drinks, Preserves and Garnishes

Commercial brands of drinks and preserves cannot hold a candle to the homemade variety but can be processed for a particular need. This chapter offers you both. Garnishing boldly but with understanding is also an essential for soft options cuisine. Here are basic recipes for the store cupboard and instructions for the ultimate in garnishes and decorations, designed to make non-chew food seductive and stimulating to the appetite.

DRINKS

Barley Water
This bears very little relation to commercial barley water. It is useful for people who are unwell and cannot take solid food but who need something stronger than just plain water.

2oz (50g) pearl barley	thinly pared rind of ½ lemon
water	1pt (600ml) boiling water from
3 teaspoons caster sugar	the kettle

Method: Put the barley into a small pan and cover with cold water. Bring to the boil and continue boiling for 2 more minutes. Strain in a fine mesh sieve. Put the prepared barley into a jug with the sugar and lemon rind. Pour in the boiling water and cover with a saucer.

Leave to steep and grow cold. Strain through a fine mesh sieve. Use as a drink, diluted with water to taste. Store in the fridge and use within a few days.

Egg Nog (serves 1)
An old-fashioned tonic.

1 white of egg
1 tablespoon brandy

1 tablespoon single cream
caster sugar to taste

Method: Whisk the egg white to a stiff froth. Mix brandy, cream and sugar in a tumbler. Carefully stir in the egg white and serve. (Not for people on an alcohol-free diet due to medication.)

Homemade Lemonade
Peel rind from a lemon (thinly) into fine strips. Put into a jug with the juice of 2 lemons. Sprinkle in a tablespoon of caster sugar and pour in 1pt (600ml) boiling water from the kettle. Leave to stand until cold. Strain through a fine mesh sieve and dilute to taste with water as required. Add a little more sugar if preferred. Store in the fridge and use within 3 days.

JAM AND MARMALADE SPREADS

Only jam without pips or pieces of fruit is suitable. One fruit pip embedding in the gum or under a dental plate can ruin a meal and be excruciatingly painful.

Some jams can be bought as jelly jams. They will have been strained to remove all pips. However, they are not always easy to come by and are rather limited in variety. Bramble, black- and redcurrant and raspberry are the most likely ones. If making jam yourself at home you will obviously be able to enjoy a wider variety (see chapter 12 for recipes).

It is possible to purée commercially made jams which contain pieces of fruit—for example, apricot, plum, damson, cherry. Put the contents of the pot into the liquidiser and blend. Spread the jam on a dinner plate and remove any lumps which have escaped the blade. Spoon what is left back into the pot and store in the fridge.

Commercially made jams which include pips can be used if put through a fine mesh sieve. Only a small amount of jam will result if there are lots of pips, as in raspberry, loganberry or blackberry.

If strawberry jam without the tiny pips is required, you will need to press it through a fine mesh sieve lined with a piece of muslin. As the joy of strawberry jam is in the whole strawberries, the point of it is rather lost. You might prefer to consider a fresh strawberry spread.

Hull, then peel about four large strawberries so that all the pips are removed (see p. 40 for details). Mash the remaining fruit on a plate using a fork. Sprinkle with sugar to taste and use immediately instead of jam. Although there are no whole strawberries in it the taste is wonderful.

Raspberries can be mashed and put through a fine mesh sieve to remove pips. Sweeten to taste and use freshly made instead of jam.

Marmalade

Either use jelly marmalade or spread marmalade on a plate and remove the shreds of orange. If you have the patience, pulverise the shreds in a pestle and mortar and put back into the pot with what is left on the plate. Stir well and store in the fridge.

Bear in mind that for some people the shreds of peel are what marmalade is about. If you can find or make marmalade with soft shreds it should respond to the liquidiser. Put the whole pot in and blend. Spread on a dinner plate and pick out any remaining shreds. Pot and store in the fridge.

You will find recipes for robust jelly-type marmalades on the following pages.

JELLY MARMALADES

The method is the same for all three marmalades which are made in quite a different way from the usual kind with shreds of rind. Buy the waxed circles, cellophane lids and labels from stationers or supermarkets.

Orange Jelly Marmalade (makes about 5lbs (2½kg))

1lb (450g) Seville or bitter oranges	3lbs (1kg 150g) granulated sugar
3pts (1½litres) water	juice of 1 lemon

Method: Shred half the peel from the oranges using a sharp knife on a board. Make the shreds as fine as possible. Put the other half of the peel, in large pieces, into a piece of muslin and tie to make a bag. In a second muslin bag put the shredded peel, pips, pith and orange pulp. Overnight soak the two bags and the shreds of peel in the water (use a large saucepan). Next day simmer very gently for an hour. Discard the 2 bags. Put in the sugar and lemon juice. Stir over a gentle heat until the sugar has completely dissolved. Turn up the heat, bring to the boil and continue until it will set. Test after 3 to 5 minutes. To do this, take pan off the heat and put a little of the marmalade on a saucer. Allow it to grow cold. Push it with your finger. If it wrinkles it is ready. If it is not, test again after 10 minutes (total) at the boil. When you are satisfied it is at setting point, pour into hot, clean and dry jars. If you tap the jars while filling them, air bubbles will come to the top. Put on the waxed circles immediately. Cover and wait until cooled to put on a label with the name and date. Store in a cool, dry and dark place.

NOTE: If the jelly boils too long it will *never* set.

Lemon Jelly Marmalade (makes just over 3lbs (1½kg))

3 large lemons   2½lbs (1¼kg) granulated sugar
2½pts (1 litre 400ml) water

Method: Make as for Orange Jelly Marmalade but without the extra juice of a lemon.

Lime Jelly Marmalade (makes just over 3lbs (1½kg))

1lb (450g) limes   2½lbs (1¼kg) granulated sugar
2½pts (1 litre 400ml) water

Method: Make as for Orange Jelly Marmalade but without the extra juice of a lemon.

JELLY JAMS

Raspberry Jelly Jam

2lbs (1kg) raspberries   granulated sugar
½ pt (300ml) water

Method: Simmer fruit and water until soft. Put into a piece of muslin and tie to make a bag. Suspend over a large bowl so that the juice drips out, preferably overnight. Measure the juice. For each pint (600ml) weigh out 1lb (450g) sugar. Put into a saucepan and heat while you stir until all the sugar has dissolved. Boil quickly until set (see Orange Jelly Marmalade regarding testing). Pour into clean, dry jars, put on waxed discs, cover and leave to grow cold. Store in a cool, dry, dark place.

Strawberry Jelly Jam

Strawberries are low in the pectin required to set jam, so lemon juice is added.

2lb (1kg) prepared strawberries (washed and hulled)

4 tablespoons water
granulated sugar

Method: Put the strawberries into a saucepan with the water and simmer until tender. Strain through a muslin bag (as for Raspberry Jelly Jam). Measure the juice and allow the juice of 2 lemons and 1lb (450g) sugar per pint (600ml) of juice. Put in with the strawberry juice and boil quickly until it will set (see Orange Jelly Marmalade regarding testing). Pour into clean, dry jars; put on waxed discs, cover and leave to grow cold. Store in a cool, dry, dark place.

NOTE: Do not expect this jelly to have the brilliant red colour of commercial strawberry jam.

Lemon Curd

Homemade lemon curd is a real treat, nothing like the yellow gunge of most commercial varieties. Eat spread generously on soft bread with the crusts cut off.

8oz (225g) granulated sugar
4oz (100g) unsalted butter, cut into small pieces
finely grated yellow rind of 3 lemons without the white pith

2 eggs
juice of 2½ lemons

Method: Have ready a pan or basin over a pan of simmering water. Put the sugar, butter, lemon rind and juice into the top pan. Cook, stirring from time to time, until the sugar and butter have melted. Beat the eggs well and add to the pan. Stir well and continue cooking until the mixture will coat the back of a wooden spoon. Pour into clean, dry jars and seal as for Orange Jelly Marmalade (p. 193).

CHUTNEYS

Soft options solutions for bought brands

Put two heaped tablespoons in a mini-chopper. Process. Spoon into a small dish. Pick out any pieces which are still solid. Either discard or chop finely with a knife, on a board, or pulverise in a pestle and mortar and stir back into the chutney. Larger amounts can be made and put back into the jar.

HOMEMADE CHUTNEYS

Smooth Date and Apple Chutney

½ medium onion
2 teaspoons sunflower oil
2 cooking apples, peeled, cored and grated
3 tablespoons wine vinegar

5 dates, stoned and finely chopped
¼ level teaspoon ground ginger
3 pinches fine pepper
brown sugar to taste

Method: Fry the onion in the oil for 4 minutes, while you stir. Add all other ingredients and a little water. Bring to the boil, stirring. Put the lid on the saucepan and simmer over a low heat for about 15 minutes. Allow to cool a little, then blend in a liquidiser. When cold, put into a clean jam jar and store covered in the fridge. Eat within a few days.

Smooth Dried Apricot Chutney

4oz (100g) dried apricots
2 heaped tablespoons sultanas
2 teaspoons sunflower oil
1 medium onion, finely chopped
4 tablespoons wine vinegar

finely grated rind of 1 orange
juice of 1 orange
4 good pinches cinnamon
¼ teaspoon made French mustard
brown sugar to taste

Method: Soak the apricots and sultanas overnight in cold water. Fry the onion in the oil for 4 minutes, while you stir. Add all other ingredients including the drained, chopped fruit and bring to the boil. Lower the heat and simmer for 10 minutes or until the apricots are soft. If it is turning out too dry, add a little water. Allow to cool. Blend in a liquidiser and turn into a clean jar. Store covered in the fridge and eat within a few days.

GARNISHES

For soft options food garnish boldly, making it obvious the garnish is not for eating. Long spikes of chives, large sprigs of parsley and watercress, slices of orange and lemon, nasturtium flowers, pansy flowers, baby spinach, lettuce and celery leaves, tomato 'roses', radish 'flowers', delicate fennel leaves, onion brushes, lemon or tomato waterlilies, lemon, orange or lime twists—the list is long and varied.

While some need little attention and can be just placed with food, others must be engineered. Here are a few simple but effective ones.

196

Tomato Roses

Using a small sharp knife, peel a tomato continuously as you would an apple. The result should be a long strip with curving edges. Roll up to form a red rose. See Diagram A.

Spring Onion Brushes

Have ready a bowl of iced water. Trim the green top of a spring onion. Cut off the white part. Use a sharp knife to shred the green but leave 1in (2.5cm) at the base. Leave in the iced water. The shreds will open out and go into curls. A rather impressive, flamboyant garnish. See Diagram B.

Radish Flowers

Trim radishes. Make deep cuts with a sharp knife to halfway down in a star, all crossing in the centre. Put into iced water to open them out. See Diagram C.

Water Lily Lemon

Take a sharp knife with a good point and cut in a zigzag line round the 'waist' of a lemon, pushing the point right into the centre of the fruit. When your zigzag joins up, pull the two halves apart. See Diagram D. Also use for oranges (small), limes and tomatoes. If necessary, cut off the ends flat to make a base so that the fruit will stand up.

Twists

Cut a thin slice from a lemon, orange or cucumber. Make a cut from the outside to the centre. Twist one half towards you and the other half away. See Diagram E.

Chives Fan

Line up several chives stalks on a chopping board so that the tops are all in line or in a curve, as neatly as you can. Cut off in a line about 3in. (7.5cm) down or longer. Arrange in a fan quite close together. See Diagram F.

What to garnish

Fish—lemon or orange twist or water lily lemon, cucumber twists, tomato rose, spring onion brush, fennel leaves.
Savoury cakes—chives fan, parsley or watercress sprigs.
Sandwiches—radish flowers, parsley or watercress sprigs, tomato rose, spring onion brush, baby spinach leaves, lettuce heart leaves, nasturtium or pansy flowers, celery leaves.

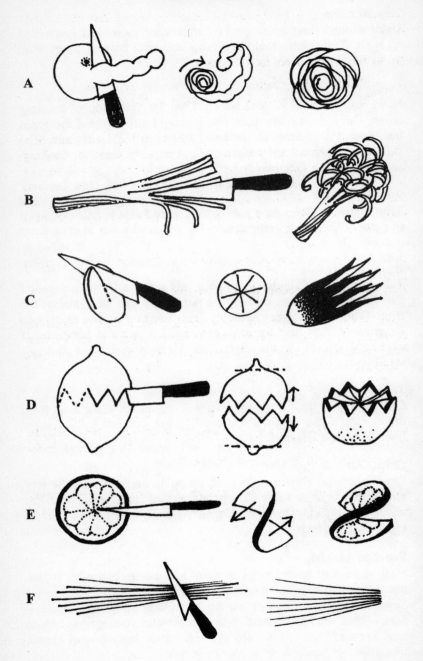

Salads—chives fan, celery leaves, lemon and cucumber twists, radish flowers.

Decorations for cakes and desserts

3 tablespoons highly coloured
fruit juice or flavoured water
(see below)

1 tablespoon cornflour
sugar to taste

Method: Put the juice-water into a small pan with the cornflour. Mix well and bring to the boil while stirring vigorously. Continue cooking for a minute and take off the heat. Sweeten to taste. Spoon on to a plate, spread flat with a knife and leave to set. When cold, cut into small shapes with a knife (squares, diamonds, triangles) or with tiny cutters (stars, circles, etc.) Arrange on top of water icing before it sets and they will stick on.

Fruit juices—orange, raspberry, redcurrant, fruits of the forest, green grapes.
Flavours—coffee, cocoa, drinking chocolate.

NOTE: If the colours are not bright enough, add a little extra edible colouring. If you cannot entertain the supermarket variety try your local health store or make your own (see p. 42). Avoid violent, dark colours. Pastel tints are always pretty and will not offend.

Chocolate decoration
Finely grate a bar of chocolate. Either use cooking chocolate or good-quality eating chocolate. Plain, milk or white are available. Sprinkle over whipped cream or water icing. This always looks attractive and will just melt in the mouth.

Other decorations to use are obvious, non-edible ones—candles, plastic or paper leaves, paper frills, etc.

APPENDICES

MAIN MEAL SUGGESTIONS (numbers in brackets refer to chapters)

Salad (8) with:
egg mayonnaise
soft meat slices (9)
cold skinless pork sausages (5)
sardines
tuna
tinned salmon
fresh poached salmon (9)
prawns in mayonnaise

Puréed vegetables with savoury cakes (9)
cod and sauce
tuna and sauce
sardine and sauce
bean, nut and cheese and sauce
nut and sauce or gravy
cheese and sauce
ham and cheese and sauce
TVP and gravy
chicken and gravy
beef and gravy

lamb and gravy
pork and gravy
fresh steaks and gravy, fried onions
fresh lamb and gravy
fresh pork and gravy
see also (12) for salmon and asparagus, pheasant and grouse

Pizza (9)

Curry and chopped rice or couscous (9)
egg
vegetarian style
meat

Pastas (4, 6 and 9)
soft lasagne with green salad
soft bacon and egg pasta

Potato-topped pies with puréed vegetables (9)
cottage (beef)
shepherd's (lamb)
chicken
TVP
fish

Fish and puréed vegetables (9)
baked
poached
quick fish pie

Scrambled eggs (5) with:
puréed spinach, carrot and potato
vegetable terrine

Omelettes with salad or puréed vegetables (5 and 9)

Cheese
leek and potato pie (8)
leeks in cheese sauce (8)
cauliflower cheese (8)
egg Florentine (5 and 8)

SOFT OPTIONS

Meat
beef with ginger, stir-fry vegetables and rice (9)
pork sausages, tomatoes, chips and fried egg (5 and 9)

All-in-one dinners (9)
beef
lamb
TVP (8)
pork
chicken
See also (9) for how to process ordinary roast dinners.

CONVERSION TABLES

Liquid Measures
The average UK tea cup contains ¼pt (150ml). The American measuring cup is two-fifths of a UK pint as the American pint is slightly smaller than a UK pint (UK pint = 20fl oz, American pint = 16fl oz).

Solid Measures

American cup conversions
1 cup breadcrumbs = 4oz (100g)
1 cup butter, margarine = 8oz (225g)
1 cup cheese, grated = 4oz (100g)
1 cup couscous = 6½oz (175g)
1 cup flour = 4oz (100g)
1 cup lentils = 6½oz (175g)
1 cup caster sugar = 7oz (200g)

Spoon conversions
½oz flour = 1 level tablespoon
1oz flour = 1 heaped tablespoon
1oz sugar = 1 level tablespoon
½oz butter = 1 levelled off tablespoon
1oz jam = 1 level tablespoon

USEFUL ADDRESSES

Automatic bread bakery (with advice service)
Panasonic Test and Development Kitchen, Panasonic UK Ltd.,
Willoughby Road, Bracknell, Berks. RG12 8PP.
Tel: 0134 886 2108. Fax: 0134 485 3217

Kitchen equipment by mail order
Robust, quality, no-nonsense equipment.
Divertimenti (Mail Order) Ltd., PO Box 6611, London SW15 2WG.
Tel: 0181 246 4300

Fan ovens
In this book oven temperatures and baking times are given for conventional gas and electric ovens. For information on converting the settings and baking times for fan ovens, see p. 42.

Index

absorption 15
alcohol 42
antioxidants 15
apples 149—50
automatic breadmakers 37

barley water 191
beef with ginger 143
biscuits 39
black treacle 53
blancmange 147
bran 53
bread 46—62
  baked loaves 52
  baking 51
  filling tins 51
  finishing 51
  kneading 49
  knocking back 50
  proving 50
  rolls 52
  slapping down 51
  soft loaves/rolls
    brown 59
    half and half 56
    malted 58
    multigrain, quick 61
    oat 57
    rye 55
    white 60
    wholewheat 55
  storage 52
  yeast for 48
bread and milk 74
bread flours, shopping for 54
breakfasts 70—84
breakfast foods, typical 74—5
building skills 44
bumble 190

cakes 160—6
  celebration, soft 172
  chocolate sponge 165
  cup cakes 161—2
  gingerbread 163
  gugelhopf 163
  light sponge 164
  Madeira 162
  orange 162
  sponge gâteau 171
  Victoria sponge 165
calories 8
cauliflower cheese 122
cheese straws 99
chewing 7, 42
chewing problems 21—2
chip butties 189
chipolatas 169
chips, fried 119
  baked 119
chocolate dessert 148
chocolate mousse 171
chocolates 175
chutney, smooth
  date and apple 196
  dried apricot 196
colourings 42
cooking equipment 28—37
  chopping knife 28
  juicers 35
  liquidiser 31
  mezzaluna 29
  mini chopper 30
  mouli 30
cooking techniques for soft options
    38—45
couscous 66
cuisine, soft options 10
curry 143

INDEX

beef and vegetable 144
egg 144
vegetarian style 143

decoration for cakes/desserts 199
desserts: *see* puddings
diet
 balanced 19
 basic balanced 23
 mixed 12
 sensible 17
 soft 9
digestion 11
dinners
 all-in-one 132
  beef 133
  chicken 135
  lamb 133
  pork 134
 processing roast 129
dried fruit 39
dumplings 68

eating
 comfortable 25
 pleasure in 18
egg custard, baked 158
egg nog 192
eggs
 baked 76
 cooked 25
 Florentine 123
 fried 76
 omelettes 77
 poached 76
equipment 28—37
Eve's pudding 153—4

fan ovens 42
feeding 26—7
fibre 15
fish
 baked 125
 fried in crumbs 126
 pie, quick 127
 poached 126
 preparation 125
flours
 barley 52
 plain white 52
 rye 53
 soya 53
 stoneground brown 53
 strong brown bread 53
 strong white bread 53
food
 fancies 25
 minimum intake 20
 safety 45

folding 43
fruit
 Alaska 167
 crumble 154
 fresh, stewed 146
 jelly 148
 on bread 156
 salad 145
 snow 152

garnishes 196
gelatine 24
gravy separator 36

hygiene 25

icing, Royal 176
 water 166

jam
 raspberry jelly 194
 strawberry jelly 195
juices
 fresh 79—82
 from canned fruit 82
 from frozen fruit 83
 from stewed fruit 83

leek and potato pie 122
leek in cheese sauce 122
lemon curd 195
lemonade 192
listeria 25
loaves 47

main meal suggestions 200—2
main meals 122—4, 125—44
malnutrition 16
malt extract 53
marmalade
 lemon jelly 194
 orange jelly 193
marzipan, soft 124
mayonnaise
 cooked 92
 egg-free 92
 using 24
 with cooked egg 92
meat slices, soft 130—2
meringue
 cooked, soft 165
 hot fruit meringue 155
milk, dried 53
minerals 14—15

nutrients 13
nutrition 11—18
 poor 16—17

oats, rolled 53
orange teabread 165
overeating 13

packed meals 178—9
pancakes 67
pasta
  brown 63
  cooking dried 63
  cooking noodles 64
  for tiny squares 64
  making tiny noodles 64
  soft lasagne 128
  spaghetti Bolognese: *see* sauces
  verdi (green) 65
pastry 38
  biscuit 67
pepper 43
pie, preparation for serving 38
pips 40, 70
pizza 127—8
porridge 73
  quick oat 73
  rice 73
potato-topped pies 135—7
presentation 43
puddings/desserts
  baked apples 150
    bananas 150
  blancmanges 147
  bread and butter 156
  chocolate dessert 148
  coffee and walnut dessert 148
  Eve's pudding 153
  fresh fruit salad 145
  fruit
    crumble 154
    fool 171
    jelly 148
    meringue, hot 155
    on bread 156
    snow 152
  lilac pears 151
  Queen of puddings 159
  rice fruit dessert 152
  scented pears 151
  steamed fruit pudding 157
  steamed sponge 158
  stewed apple 148
  stewed fresh fruit 146

recipe books 44
remedies 27
rolls 47

salad dressings 90—3
salad oils 91
salads 109—14
  processing 112

table 110
  vegetables 39
sandwiches 180—8
  asparagus 183
  banana 182
    and cream 182
  beef 186
  beef dripping and juices 187
  bloater 187
  cheese 184
    and beetroot 185
    and chives 184
    and date 184
    and pickle 184
    and tomato 184
    and walnut 184
  crab 187
  cream cheese 184
  curried egg 183
  egg 182
    and cress 183
    and parsley 183
    and watercress 183
  extra special 177
  fillings for, soft 182—8
  ham and egg 183
  kipper 188
  lobster 177
  meat slices, soft 186
  pilchards 188
  prawn 187
  salmon 185
    and shrimp 185
    and cucumber 185
  sardine 185
    and tomato 185
  smoked salmon 177
  tuna and mayonnaise 185
    and salad 186
  watercress 183
sauces
  asparagus 86
  basic white 85
  béchamel 86
  cheese 86
  cucumber and lemon 86
  egg 86
  for pasta
    Bolognese 88
    salsa di carne 87
  mushroom 86
  onion 86
  parsley 86
  pesto 107
  soy 94
  tomato 86, 89
    and herb 86
  tuna and tomato 89
savoury cakes

INDEX

bean, nut and cheese 140
beef 139
cheese 141
chicken 139
cod 138
fresh meat 141–2
  lamb 141
  pork 142
  steak 141
ham and cheese 141
lamb 139
nut 140
pork 140
sardine 139
tuna 139
TVP 140
savoury cakes, luxury
  grouse 167
  pheasant 169
  salmon and asparagus 168
seeds 40
shakes 83–4
  banana 84
  breakfast 83
  pineapple 84
size of meals 27
skinless pork sausages 78
slices 188–9
snacks 190
soft meat slices 130–2
soup accompaniments 95
soups
  asparagus 167
  baked bean 105
  carrot 99
  celery 98
    and celeriac 98
    cream of 98
  chicken 106
  cucumber 104
  fish 105
  leek and potato 100
  lentil 104
  minestrone 101
  mushroom 97
    cream of 98
  onion, clear 103
  pepper and tomato 97
  split pea 105
  tomato 96
    fresh 96
  vegetable
    autumn 103

broth 101
  spring 102
  summer 102
  thick 102
  vichyssoise 100
  watercress, thick 99
    thin 99
starters
  avocado and orange 106
  chicken liver pâté 108
  pawpaw with prawns 107
  pesto 107
  prawn cocktail 108
steaming 41
stock
  soya 94
  vegetable 90
stuffing, soft 68

teeth 7
tomatoes, special preparation 40
trifle
  Black Forest 175
  fruit, sherry 175

vegans 12
vegetables (*see also* salads)
  broad beans 116
  broccoli 115
  Brussels sprouts 114
  cauliflower 116
  cooked 114
  French beans 115
  greens 114
  leeks 115
  mushrooms 116
  onions 116
  peas 115
  potatoes 117–18
  root 120
  runner beans 115
  stir-fry 121
vegetarian dishes 122–4
vegetarians 20–1
vermicelli: *see* pasta
vinaigrettes 91

water 15
wheatgerm 53

yeast 48
yoghurt, flavoured 71–2